Feeding the Flock

Restaurants and Churches

You'd

Stand

in

Line

For

by *Russell Chandler*

An Alban Institute Publication

Unless otherwise indicated, Scripture quotations are from The Holy Bible: *New International Version*, copyright © 1973, 1978, 1984, by permission of Zondervan Bible Publishers. Scripture quotations identified NASB are from the New American Standard Bible, copyright © 1960, 1962, 1963, 1968, 1971, 1972, 1973, 1975, 1977 by The Lockman Foundation; used by permission.

The publications program of the Alban Institute is assisted by a grant from Trinity Church, New York.

Library of Congress Catalog Number 97-78132
ISBN 1-56699-196-X

To my cousin, Walter C. McDowell,
restaurateur and chef par excellence,
who never met a recipe he couldn't improve.

CONTENTS

"It's just your imagination!"

With these words we were chided as children into dismissing and "dissing" our imaginative powers. With these words we learned not to take our imagination seriously. No wonder the church has such an imagination deficit.

Russell Chandler believes it is time for the church to take back the imaginal and take seriously the creative. In the face of a crisis-level drift and atrophy of spiritual imagination, Chandler presents us with a book that practices what it preaches.

The most impressive feature of this title is the way Chandler excels in getting our minds to "jump the rails" in search of new insights into how to do church in postmodern culture. He is not the first to use eating rituals in such a creative way. Nietzsche used food metaphors for philosophy, art, and psychology, and even for his attack on Christian theology itself.

But Chandler has understood how bread is at the heart of daily life and routines. In eighteenth-century Paris, for example, a table liturgy was a bread ritual. The bread was examined at mealtimes for its baker's mark. Then the host would take the tip of a knife and mark the bread with the sign of a cross before breaking and eating it.

Chandler performs a similar ritual with our eating habits and restaurant habitations. He picks them up, examines them for their unique signatures, then shows us how we can learn from them to make the sign of the cross for upcoming generations.

His methodology is the same as that of Leonardo da Vinci when he was serving as an apprentice. Da Vinci's father, Ser Piero, presented him with a shield and a challenge: paint something on the shield. Son

Leonardo decided to paint for his father something that would, as he put it, "terrify the enemy." He collected in his room the makings of his model: "lizards, newts, crickets, serpents, butterflies, grasshoppers, bats and other strange animals." Out of the mix of these creatures he fashioned a monster, horrible and horrifying, which released a poisonous brimstone breath and ignited the air into flame. When his father came to pick up the shield, he "received a great shock" and almost fell over backwards with fright. To Ser Piero, his son's creation appeared "nothing short of a miracle."[1]

Da Vinci calls this his "strategy of combination." He made imaginary animals out of real ones. One of Da Vinci's biographers, Giorgio Vasari, says that "On the back of a most strange lizard, found by a vine-dresser of the Belvedere, Leonardo attached wings made of scales taken from other lizards, helped by quicksilver, which as the lizard moved, quivered with the motion. He then made it eyes, a horn, and a beard, tamed it and, keeping it in a box, he showed it to friends to make them flee for fear."

What is the essence of creativity? What releases the powers of the imagination? According to one study of fifty-eight geniuses, including Einstein, Picasso, and Mozart, *all* their breakthroughs occurred when "two or more opposites were conceived simultaneously, existing side-by-side–as equally valid, operative and true." The research report concludes: "In an apparent defiance of logic or physical possibility, the creative person consciously [embraced] antithetical elements and developed these into integrated entities and creations."[2]

Imagination expert Bryan Mattimore says that this method of taking characteristics already present in nature and mixing them together in new and fresh ways is the essence of genius and the heart of imagination itself.

It is also the essence of Russell Chandler's audacious and original attempt to help the church climb out of self-made bunkers and enter the twenty-first century. By grinding church and culture together with a single pestle of mission, he shows that we are not just what we eat but how we eat.

We can't go back to earlier ways of doing church. We can only go forward. We will never know how bread used to taste because the bread kneaders in times past would work so hard and sweat so profusely that the dough was watered with their sweat, giving it a unique flavor. We can only enjoy and evaluate the bread baked by today's cooks and ovens.

The U.S. motto "E Pluribus Unum" (From Many, One) actually comes from a recipe book: white cheese is gradually mixed with a variety of green herbs until the colors merge.[3] From the mixing and matching of many diverse strains comes one powerful recipe book in how to do church. It's an imaginative tour de force.

Leonard I. Sweet
Drew University Theological School

NOTES
1. The story is told by Bryan W. Mattimore, *99% Inspiration* (New York: AMACOM, 1994), 66.
2. The report is chronicled in Richard Tanner Pascale, *Managing on the Edge: How the Smartest Companies Use Conflict to Stay Ahead* (NY: Simon and Schuster, 1990), 110.
3. Andrew Dalby, *Siren Feasts: A History of Food and Gastronomy in Greece* (NY: Routledge, 1997).

Appetizers

Several years ago I was on a writing assignment in Portland, Oregon, for *The Los Angeles Times*. At dinner time, I strolled along the Willamette River waterfront looking for a good place to eat. Most of the restaurants had only a few customers. At best, several appeared moderately busy.

Except for one: a line snaked out the door and halfway down the block. Obviously, the Harborside was *the* place to dine! It was a predominantly Generation X Yuppie crowd, and I suspected the Harborside was as much an after-work gathering place as it was noted for its food.

That Portland experience got me thinking: What makes people wait in line for up to an hour or more to be seated in a particular restaurant while half a dozen other cafes in the immediate vicinity are half-empty?

I pondered that question while I ate a delicious leg-of-lamb dinner in one of the less busy restaurants rather than wait forty-five minutes to be seated at the Harborside. I decided good food and prompt service in themselves may not be enough to attract and hold a capacity clientele.

And so was born the Russ Chandler "Theory of Restaurant Success." It's simple: The word gets around that Cafe XXX has really good food and an attractive ambiance. People invite their friends. Before long, it's perceived as *the* place to go, the place to schmooze, to take your date or spouse or kids; then that restaurant's clientele grows exponentially. It's just an application of the old adage: Nothing succeeds like success.

Then I started applying my restaurant theory to churches. Yes, the same principles work there, too, I decided. The popular churches, the ones that draw crowds, grow even larger and attract a disproportionate share of the area's churchgoing public. Meanwhile, other houses of worship in the same neighborhood—despite good preaching and attempts to be friendly—often languish or fail to grow.

If you want a good meal, go to a busy restaurant. If you want a fulfilling, satisfying church experience, visit a busy, happy congregation.

St. Alban's—The "In" Place for Teens

In the city where I grew up, almost all the important kids from my high school went to a particular church youth group. The word had gotten around and this group pulled kids from families who attended other churches. I'm sure the other youth groups were interesting and spiritual and all that, but the jocks and cheerleaders—the "in" kids—went to St. Albans. So, guess where I went, too.

Cut to Bowling Green, Kentucky, and Cracker Barrel Old Country Store. (Actually it's a restaurant and a gift shop combined in one building.)

On a trip to the Southeast with my wife, Marjorie Lee (she goes by ML), I once again saw my Theory of Restaurant Success in action. Waiting time at the Bowling Green Cracker Barrel that night was about forty minutes. Nearby restaurants were filled—with empty tables.

We waited at Cracker Barrel. It was worth it. In fact, we ate at Cracker Barrels during the next two days of our trip. Why take the chance of being disappointed when you've found a really good thing?

We'll come back to the Cracker Barrel in a later chapter, and savor this chain's succulent secrets of success.

At the time I stood in line at the Cracker Barrel, I was buzzing around the country giving church leadership seminars. I talked about trends in society and religion, about preparing for the future, about visioning, goal setting, marketing, and church growth. (Much of the impetus for my seminars on church leadership for the twenty-first century sprang from my book, *Racing Toward 2001: The Forces Shaping America's Religious Future*, published in 1992 by Zondervan.)

I began to apply restaurant patterns to models of church leadership. Using a blackboard or flip chart, I elicited parallels from the church leaders in my audiences. It was fun—and provocative. "What makes a good restaurant?" I would ask. The list grew as people told about where they liked to eat and why. (This especially commands good attention

PEANUTS is reprinted by permission of United Features Syndicate, Inc.

SUNDAY, JANUARY 30, 1994

just before the lunch or dinner hour!) I would continue: "Can you make a parallel between this restaurant and an effective, thriving church?"

"What makes a good restaurant go downhill?" I asked. Reasons were listed on the chart. By now, most everyone would be getting into the game. I could almost see lightbulbs turning on in their minds as rather obvious, yet often overlooked parallels emerged: visioning, goals, programs, building plans, location, staffing, teaching. All these and more were being rethought in light of the restaurant analogy.

And that's just what should happen when you read *Feeding the Flock: Restaurants and Churches You'd Stand in Line For*. If you like eating and enjoy good restaurants, as I do, then you'll find plenty of food for mind and soul. And if you love God's church as I do, perhaps you'll have a full plate of spiritual food to serve up to a hungry world when you put down this book. We don't have to queue up to receive salvation through Jesus Christ, of course. But if we did, it would be worth standing in line for.

Why You Should Read This Book

So, come along. Enjoy a mouth-watering gastronomic tour of more than twenty intriguing and popular restaurants from Baltimore to Bowling Green to Berkeley.

You'll understand why

* some restaurants become extremely successful
* while others decline and fall.

You—and those you work and worship with—will be invited to interact with creative parallels to churches. You can gain practical insights into

* why thriving churches operate under these same principles
* and how you can apply them in your own leadership situations.

In sum, through lighthearted yet solid fare, *Feeding the Flock: Restaurants and Churches You'd Stand in Line For* honors Jesus' command to his disciples: "If you love me, feed my sheep" (John 21:15-18).

Who Should Read This Book

The primary audience for *Feeding the Flock* is the ordained and lay leadership of America's churches and ministries. And it's designed to appeal to the entire religious community as well because it's entertaining reading, not preachy yet highly informative and motivational.

I've designed the book for individuals as well as for study and planning groups, staff, boards and agencies, and teachers. The book is intended to stimulate original thinking and enable readers to come up with their own personal or group vision and strategies.

Here's a sampling of special guests I've invited to join me inside *Feeding the Flock*:

- restaurant customers = church members, occasional pew warmers/ attenders
- restaurant owners/directors of operations = denominational honchos, church trustees
- restaurant managers = senior pastors, boards, business managers
- chefs/cooks = elders, deacons, teachers
- waiters, waitresses, bartenders = other staff and volunteer leaders
  – the team players who make the church function from day to day
- future restaurant staff = seminarians, pastors in training, seminary faculty

Getting the Most out of *Feeding the Flock*

1. Take notes as you ponder the questions in the church track (the second half of each chapter), and follow up with the action items suggested there. Involve the appropriate decision-makers whenever possible.

2. *Feeding the Flock* is most likely to help leaders change if you use it in a group, at a staff meeting, or at a board retreat. Assign chapters to be read in advance.

3. Make the book required reading for every new staff person and each new officer.

4. Use it at training sessions.

5. Fill out the charts in chapter 11, "The Cracker Barrel Concept," and chapter 12, "Tough Act to Swallow: What Sours a Good Restaurant? or a Good Church?" and discuss the results in light of your particular leadership role(s). Then post your charts for further dialog and implementation.

6. After members of a group have read *Feeding the Flock*, ask them to list the most significant ideas they gleaned overall. Record and prioritize those things you aren't doing yet but could in the future.

7. Agree on an action plan. In other words, don't just think or talk about it—do it! As motivational trainer Albert Koons once said: "The venture must follow the vision. It's not enough to stare up the steps; we must step up the stairs."

Warning! Read This Label Before Serving!

Yes, yes, I know. This is a controversial book—at least in some circles. Perhaps you said to yourself when you picked it up: "But a restaurant is *not* a church!" I agree. And it's certainly not my intention to demean or trivialize Christ's church. So in the introduction, I talk about some of the differences between restaurants and churches—especially the disparate understandings of motivation, "success," and rewards.

You'll find that, for all the dissimilarities, there are many surprising parallels. A church is *not* a restaurant, but Jesus did talk a lot about spiritual (as well as physical) food. And as we'll see in chapter 13, "Food and the Bible," he often taught about the rules of table fellowship.

Why Churches Should Pay Attention to Restaurants

*For the kingdom of God is not eating and drinking, but righteous-
ness and peace and joy in the Holy Spirit.*

(Romans14:17 NASB)

The anticipated objection is, "But a restaurant is *not* a church, and a
church is *not* a restaurant!" Although the point is obvious, the ideas,
values, and feelings behind this criticism need to be taken seriously.
Some may say that even making a comparison between restaurants and
churches is dangerous because doing so demeans or trivializes the church.
In fact, the danger of trivialization is pointed out in the subtitle of an
excellent book, *The Trivialization of God: The Dangerous Illusion of
a Manageable Deity*. The author, Donald W. McCullough, president of
San Francisco Theological Seminary, puts us on guard against "foolish"
religion and "silly" spirituality. Surely there is an abundance of both
these days.

I also pay attention to warnings raised by that eminent church his-
torian and astute religion observer, Martin E. Marty. He comments about
church "success" in *Newsweek* magazine (August 9, 1993): "To give the
whole store away to match what this year's market says the unchurched
want is to have the people who know least about faith determine most
about its expression." And writing about Dietrich Bonhoeffer for one of
his regular columns in *The Christian Century* (May 10, 1995), Marty
says:

I had recently read four *New York Times* stories about "successful"
churches that are crowded, giddy and crossless. I am too wary to

celebrate them, too wishy-washy to criticize them and too weary to study them. But I had to wonder how one shifts from their emphasis on entertainment to Bonhoeffer's famous line in *The Cost of Discipleship*: "When Christ calls a man, he bids him come and die." Can that call come after the entertainment?

Fair enough. But remember, *Feeding the Flock* is only making an analogy, and you and I need to remember not to draw the analogy too tightly: I want us to think and act creatively about leading a church—not about turning it into a fast-food diner.

Criticizing the Church-Growth and Seeker-Sensitive Movements

Without being exhaustive (or exhausting) here, I'll try to summarize the chief arguments against the church-growth and seeker-sensitive movements. One of the best summations is found in the article, "Selling Out the House of God?" in *Christianity Today* (July 18, 1994). It includes a detailed response by Bill Hybels, pastor of Willow Creek Community Church, a megachurch near Chicago. John N. Vaughn, publisher of *Church Growth Today*, also ably summarizes criticism of the church-growth movement in his 1993 Presidential Address to the American Society for Church Growth. His published speech is titled, "The Church Growth Movement: Offense to the Cross?"

At the outset, let's agree that the worst features of American evangelicalism cannot—and should not—be defended either by analogy or by direct application. I'm talking about anti-intellectualism, crass marketing of the "pearl of great price," huckster television preachers, personality and ego-driven ministers and ministries, and religious empire-building.

And so you know where I'm coming from, I'm an evangelical Presbyterian who believes in the high authority of Scripture; the deity of Jesus Christ—God's unique and only Son; the regenerating and sanctifying power of the Holy Spirit; and the church, the body of Christ, as God's essential reconciling agent in a sinful and fallen world. I affirm the Apostles' Creed. And I believe a person receives salvation by accepting Jesus Christ as personal Savior and Lord. Forgiven of sin, one is born again into a new life in the Spirit.

But I don't consider this book the place to champion doctrine—only to assert the core beliefs, the critical and essential foundations of biblical faith.

Objections Defined

Seeker-sensitive churches are those that tailor their main services and programs to appeal to persons either unfamiliar with—or turned off by—traditional church worship. The chief concerns about seeker-sensitive churches are that:

- The essential Gospel is compromised by secular approaches and adapting messages to appeal to non-Christians.
- "Polished" entertainment, "feel-good" sermons (telling people what they want to hear), and marketing techniques subtly undermine the Gospel message.
- An attitude of "it works, so it must be right" usurps scriptural principles and the sovereignty of God.
- Success measured by financial profit and congregational size nullifies the role of faithfulness and obedience in the life of the Christian community.
- The biblical basis for church growth is replaced by:
  — audience ratings and opinion surveys;
  — demographic polls, statistical summaries, and population charts;
  — preoccupation with corporate image and celebrity status;
  — strategies grounded in secular psychology, sociology, and management methodology and philosophy.

Answering the Objections

- Seeker-sensitive churches compromise the Gospel through secular "market-driven" philosophy. Market-driven, no; Gospel-driven, yes. "Marketing" the church is not taboo if what is meant by marketing is proclaiming the Gospel—implementing the Great Commission to "make disciples of all nations" (Matthew 28:19). Marketing means techniques, not goals. Marketing the church means a method of distributing information and materials to and between churches. It is not an end in itself. Market-*oriented* is okay; market-*driven* is not.

To create or grow a church solely through secular resources without the power and presence of God is clearly not a Christian option. Methods alone cannot win the lost or disciple the saved. Only God's Spirit can ultimately accomplish this.

• Seeker-sensitive churches emphasize entertainment. Entertainment has been cited as the "watering-down factor" that cheapens the Gospel and makes no real demands on churchgoers. Jesus didn't turn wine into water. He didn't take something valuable and turn it into some-thing "cheap." But he did take what was common and turn it into something extraordinary (see John 2:6-10). Drama, contemporary Christian music and concerts, multimedia presentations—all these and more can be techniques for reaching people, but not goals or ends. They shouldn't be used merely for the sake of entertainment. Jesus didn't perform miracles to please crowds. Yet in the context of his teaching he tailored his approach to the needs and receptiveness of his audiences. The common people "heard him gladly" (Mark 12:37).

"Who was the master composer?" asks Bill Hybels. "Who created the arts? Whose idea was it to communicate the truth through a wide variety of artistic genres? I think it was God."

Yes, Christ's call to "come and die" *can* come after the "entertainment." You've got to get my attention before I'll follow you.

• Seeker-sensitive churches embrace the attitude that "it works, so it must be right"; they emphasize the numbers game and the bottom line.

Biblical values count. Members count. We count members because numerical church growth can be evidence of effective proclamation of the Gospel and biblical values. Again, numbers for the sake of numbers is not the ultimate measuring rod. Nor is the size of a budget necessarily an index of spiritual vitality or mature discipleship.

But the critics seem to deprecate vigorous growth and robust giving as if these were sure signs that the church or ministry exhibiting them is "dining with the devil" or making deadly secular compromises. Are these flourishing groups any less blessed by God than small, struggling, financially strapped organizations?

God's sovereignty and authority extend over all spheres of human interaction and management. God is Lord of business principles just as God is Lord of music and liturgy. Using management and marketing skills to grow a church or ministry does not *per se* compromise the Gospel or capitulate to modern secularism. "If it works, it must be wrong" isn't right, either.

Pastor and author Leith Anderson has said:

> The best the church has to offer is the Word of God and the best the business world has to offer is methodology. . . . The biblical world view has no essential line that divides sacred and secular or church and business. . . . The biblical world view is that they are all part of God's creation and the distinctions are functional. ("The Best Is Yet to Come," *Forum Files*, vol. 4, no. 3 [August 1994], 3-4.)

The Rev. Terry Walton, pastor of First United Methodist Church of Acworth, Georgia, chairs the denomination's Vision 2000 emphasis. He views the emphasis on numbers this way:

> People are wanting; they're hungry; and they're needy. It is a spiritual need, but sometimes in order to get to the spiritual need, you have to help them understand you care about them at the level of their human need before they will give you the time of day. ("Vision 2000 Emphasis Helps Georgia Churches Meet Community Needs," interview with United Methodist News Service, February 27, 1995)

Vision 2000 may boost church rolls, but it isn't a numbers game: "This is not about numbers," insists Walton. "It is about being effective change agents for Christ in our communities. . . . The Gospel is the same yesterday, today and forever, but the way we communicate that had better change or we will die."

• In seeker-sensitive churches, the biblical imperative to challenge and change people is replaced by the goal of success and by merely satisfying them.

How do you define success? In a for-profit business, success is defined by the monetary bottom line, by being profitable. Restaurants succeed by acquiring and maintaining customers. And they acquire and maintain customers by pleasing, or satisfying, their guests.

The mission of Jesus Christ is to give life—abundant life—to his followers. This sense of joy and fulfillment surpasses all others. But the satisfaction and "success" are not positioned by worldly standards. The mission of the church is to change people, not merely to satisfy them. Christ's mission cuts to the heart of humanity's ultimate need—reconciliation to God.

The church's mission begins by determining and meeting people's needs, then going beyond their expressed and felt needs to challenge them with the demands of godly commitment and discipleship. When they accept the challenge, God changes them.

We may walk away from the Lord's communion table full and satisfied in a relationship of grace and intimacy. But it's not like getting up from a good meal at a restaurant: If we are not also challenged and changed men and women—disciples willing to endure the cross in an aloof and antagonistic world—then we did not truly partake in the feast Christ serves us.

Management versus Leadership

More than a few theologians are suspicious of—even hostile toward—popular expressions of the faith. In particular, they fear that success and technique will overshadow serious worship and careful theological reflection. For example, just mention a seminar on management methods for ministers, and some folks—and not just theologians—roll their eyes and say icily: "Management doesn't belong in the church. *Leadership* does."

The debate is on. "Leadership vs. Management: When Definitions Collide" is the title of a two-part series by Olan Hendrix and Jeffrey King in *Leadership Briefings*. (This newsletter on expertise in management and funding for Christian leaders is produced by Leadership Resource Group, Inc., Tempe, Arizona. See the September and October 1995 issues.)

The authors conclude that in everyday practice, the words *management* and *leadership* are almost indistinguishable. And they approvingly quote Lewis A. Allen in his book, *Management and Organization*, which says that leading is simply one of the four ingredients of management. (The other three are planning, organizing, and controlling.) When seen in that light, say Hendrix and King, leadership essentially becomes a subset of management skills. If this is so, then church leaders shouldn't bristle over the concept of church and ministry management.

But I disagree with Hendrix and King. I think it's the other way around: there's good biblical support to make management a subset of leadership (for example, see the story of Moses' appointing the judges in Exodus 18:14-26). Confusion and antiscriptural application result when we put management ahead of leadership. This is especially true when we try to manage *people*. Overall leadership is primary; the proper sequence is to *lead* people and *manage* (inanimate) things.

If we as Christian leaders train our staff and volunteers by *leading* them, then they—and we—in turn will be successful *managers* of time, facilities, activities, resources, problems, and disputes. And those we lead will themselves lead our valued guests into deeper relationships with the Lord.

Lead people, manage things.

Asking the Hard Questions

If Christianity is made too attractive and acceptable, reason those who oppose "cultural devices," then preachers in these user-friendly churches lose their cutting edge and are unable to fearlessly proclaim the whole counsel of God. In other words, in restaurant parlance, church market-eers could ask a guest, "How is your sole?" but never, "How is your *soul*?" Obviously the hard questions must be asked. The harsh reality of sin, the cross, and self-denial are integral to the Christian faith. To omit them is to proclaim an incomplete—if not defective—Gospel. Christians need more than a heaping plate of their favorite food. The whole counsel of God means consuming a balanced diet over a long period of time.

Bill Hybels says a biblically functioning community today is one with a "full-orbed approach to bringing people to Christ, assimilating them into the body of Christ, discipling them, helping them find their spiritual gifts, and sensitizing them to the needs of the world."

But as Leith Anderson points out, "the rules of yesterday have been replaced." Today, the entry point for the faith for many people is a relationship, not a program. They want an experience of the faith and a sense of connection to God before they can come to the point of real comprehension or intellectual understanding of what discipleship means. They want and need to be served before they want and need to serve.

Do not shuck off or soft-pedal the hard questions. Sin needs to be identified, confessed, and forgiven by God. Restitution is not passé. To walk the path with Jesus today is the same as it has always been: those who want to come after Jesus must deny themselves and take up their cross–daily (Matthew 16:24). Bonhoeffer was right: when Christ calls a man (or woman), he bids him come and die.

Who Pays the Price?

Our society's values are indeed 180 degrees away from those taught by Jesus Christ. But the Willow Creek model is to say, "Come as you are. Come with your BMW and your Rolex because even though you have caved in to the values of this sick culture, you still matter to God."

"And when they confess their sins and see what Christ did for them at the cross, we begin a very aggressive value-transformation program that will not stop until they go to their graves," says Hybels. To live is Christ, and to die is gain.

Perhaps, in a curious kind of trade-off, seeker-sensitive churches are making evangelism easier and discipleship harder, as growth-movement critic Os Guinness suggests in *Dining with the Devil*. But the answer is not to back away from sharing the Gospel with the millions outside the faith. Surely it is to evangelize as well as to intensify renewal within the churches. And to strengthen the discipling of those who have come to Christ. We must focus on both evangelism and discipleship, each without shortchanging the other.

To do this means paying a price—just as it does when we dine out, pick up the tab, and hand over our cash or credit card. We must pay for the benefits we have received. Commitment to Christ is costly, as Bonhoeffer so cogently and classically reminds us.

For those in leadership roles the cost of discipleship is even greater. We will share the chastisements and stripes of the Great Shepherd of the sheep. There is a price to pay if we preach the Scriptures unapologetically and challenge the prevailing counter-Kingdom values of the secular culture.

To do so is always demanding. It's often perplexing. Sometimes it's frightening. Many pastors I speak to these days are numbed by the complexities, disheartened by the apathy, and chilled by the competing, seductive voices calling their women, men, and youth to alternative altars. The heart of being able to stand in such a time is not leading—or managing—alone. It is in leading with others through team teaching, team leadership, and team vision-casting. The toll is then less draining, less exacting on our personal resources. We need to split the bill.

And please don't forget that bounteous resource, the laity. Much criticism against the seeker-sensitive approach is leveled by theological elites who distrust lay people and their ability to discern Scripture. Richard Mouw, president of Fuller Theological Seminary in Pasadena, California, addresses this perception, saying that "gifted lay people have a spiritual wisdom that is tuned to the basic rhythms of the religious quest."

Farmers and waitpersons have just as much access to God as do trained theologians and religious professionals. Theology has as much to do with families and businesses as it does with the Trinity and the sacraments. Theological reflection must employ the insights of the *entire* Christian community, Mouw asserts:

> Rather than send the laity off to do their own theology, it is important to draw them into the larger process. . . . If the laity cannot see how the "high" theology of the theologians connects with their day-to-day concerns, then they will, at best, not value the work of theologians, or, at worst, embrace a less-than-orthodox expression of the faith. ("Ending the Cold War Between Theologians and Lay People," *Christianity Today* [July 18, 1994], 29-30)

And if they don't value what is offered, they won't pick up the tab. They will not pay the price.

Mouw tells a story about a young "born-again" manager-type who refers to God as his CEO. He said God was "working to see that his special employees made a profit."

Obviously, as Mouw concludes, the man is a theological babe, if not an illiterate. Yet, says Mouw, it's "just as obvious that he had found some appropriate analogies from his own experience to capture his sense of God."

That is what I have tried to do in *Feeding the Flock: Restaurants and Churches You'd Stand in Line For*. Is this tacky theology? Maybe.

But, as Mouw points out, many of Jesus' parables could be considered a kind of "sanctified tackiness." Jesus talks about profoundly spiritual things by using images from everyday life that are familiar to his hearers: coins, loans, sheep, taxes, seeds, weeds, fields, fishing, farming, eating, drinking, and table manners.

His ultimate message, couched in everyday concepts and language, is far from tacky. It is the message of redeeming, suffering love that paid the price. He paid the wages of our sin and death by dying on the cross. He paid the price that we might share not only in his suffering, but also in his eternal glory.

Who pays the price? He did.

Who pays the price? We do.

When you and I understand what he did for us, we pay gladly. In the hope of glory.

PART 1

Succulent Success Stories

CHAPTER 1

Meet Me at Chevys
(Foster City, California)

We were to meet Tom and Debbie at Chevys at six-thirty. It was a balmy fall evening and my wife, ML, and I planned to catch the ten o'clock red-eye special to Washington, D.C., out of San Francisco International. Chevys fronted a boardwalk along the bay at Foster City, just five miles south of the airport and about fifteen miles north of where Tom and Debbie, our thirties-age son and daughter-in-law, lived and worked near the Stanford University campus.

We arrived at the restaurant on Edgewater Boulevard first and put in our name—no advance reservations are accepted. We strolled along the boardwalk and had a few minutes to size up the place before Tom and Deb joined us.

Of course, Chevys was packed on a Friday night with the young, after-work crowd. But there were lots of families, too, and a sprinkling of retirees and grandparents among the casually dressed crowd.

Several greeters stationed at the front entrance opened the doors to welcome each arriving guest. They chatted informally for a moment with the newcomers, then motioned them into the fan-shaped reception area where they could mingle with the waiting flock. We began to absorb impressions: Chevys was open to all. No discrimination, no dress code. Come as you are. Be prepared to relax, have fun. Enjoy a delicious meal.

The decor, simple but engaging, displayed a south-of-the-border motif. Artifacts and paintings portrayed the history and culture of other eras and other places. Chevys is a theme restaurant that works.

The lounge, off to one side of the reception hub, beckoned with happy-hour laughter. But many children and their parents filled the spacious dining alcoves. The ambiance seemed to say, "Kids are okay here—this is a place for the family." A clown and a jester worked the dining area, perching at each table where there were children. Blowing up brightly colored balloons, the jester deftly twisted several together, fashioning them into a custom hat, or weaving them into the shape of an animal—all to the kids' delight. As each family unit was recognized, a kind of tableside bonding took place with the employees.

Fellowship, affirmation, and celebration were key here, I decided. Laughter, balloons, and songs combined to make a warm experience. Each birthday guest was recognized and celebrated as a huge sombrero was placed on his or her head. A coterie of servers, bussers, and the clown and jester gathered round to serenade and applaud. Folks at neighboring tables enthusiastically joined in the merriment and rite of passage.

I was thinking about how all of this might apply to making families feel at home in the church when Tom and Debbie appeared at the door. Still waiting for a table, we had a chance to catch up on family news. Time passed quickly, and it seemed less than the estimated twenty minutes before we heard, "Chandler party of four, please; your table is ready." The receptionist seated us beside a large bayside window where we looked out beyond a dock to several sailboats bobbing. Seagulls swooped and squawked, arguing over territorial rights.

The "Fresh Mex Pledge"

We were hungry and the large menus quickly caught our attention. On the cover, up front, was Chevys' "mission statement"—the company pledge of "authentic made-from-scratch" Mexican food. Among other things, the Fresh Mex Pledge promises fresh, first-rate ingredients, salsa blended hourly from freshly charred tomatoes, onions, and jalapeños, and nothing out of a can. Ever.

"We even offer a kitchen tour for nonbelievers," the manager told us when he stopped by our table. We chatted about the pledge as a kind of creed, the foundation of the Chevys Mexican Restaurants' philosophy.

This chain jumped to life in California and has been growing ever more rapidly since Taco Bell (then a unit of PepsiCo Inc.) acquired it in 1993. One aspect that has made Chevys Mexican fare so popular is its crossing the border into full-service, midscale dining. Chevys' top demographic draw is young families and adults in the 25- to 49-year-old

range. We could see why Tom and Debbie felt comfortable in this atmosphere. Friendly and interracial, it reflected the diverse lifestyles and
rich ethnicity prevalent along the sprawling San Francisco Bay penin-
sula and the Silicon Valley area bracketing San Jose.

Even before ML and I read about the mouth-watering selection of
Fresh Mex described on the menu and heard our waiter recite the specials
of the day, I spied the Rube Goldberg-like tortilla *el machino* in the
center of the restaurant–a fixture at every Chevys that resembles a
toaster oven with a moving belt. You *knew* that pledge about "fresh"
was for real. We could watch the food being prepared. Trust in the
integrity of the product was created by congruence between what was
promised and what we could actually see happening. As quickly as the
piping hot, cholesterol-free tortillas rolled off the el machino production
line (every fifty-three seconds), servers scooped them into baskets and
hustled them off to patrons.

The food was reasonably priced, with a wide variety of choices. A
description of each dish listed the ingredients. You could even concoct
your own "designer plate," sampling to match individual tastes. How
about, for the calorie conscious, some ultra-thin nacho chips and a vege-
tarian bean entree? (None of us chose that; I selected chile rellenos
made from fresh poblano chilis and stuffed with fluffy Monterey jack
cheese.)

A constant refill of salsa, tortillas, and warm chips came without
our asking. And a few minutes later when our friendly server brought
our dinners, he warned us that the heaping plates were sizzling hot. The
slices of skirt steak and chicken breast, marinated in an authentic Mexican sauce and grilled over mesquite, were attractively arranged and
appetizingly presented. Time and lively conversation flew. Soon our
Fresh Mex was devoured (but I had saved just enough room for a custard
flan —one of my favorite desserts). We hugged Tom and Debbie in the
parking lot, climbed into our Ford, and headed up the busy Bayshore
Highway toward the San Francisco airport.

❖

Demographics are the data and statistics of a population group—such as geographic distribution, age, race, work, family life, income, spending, and the like. Conducting a demographic survey can help a church or business identify and concentrate on the needs of its present or future "customers" (those who use and value their services). It can also help determine the target—the strongest potential "customer" base for that operation or ministry.

Demographic tools are commonly used today, both in the restaurant industry and for denominational strategy and new church development. Some churches have specifically targeted the boomer and buster populations and have successfully blended conservative theology with a laid-back approach. The pastors wear jeans, rock replaces organ music, and members hug one another at the door. Where this style catches on—the Hope Chapel, Calvary Chapel, and Vineyard Christian Fellowship movements come to mind as examples—you're apt to find Bible-toting boomers and busters emerging from vans and sports-utility vehicles in packed parking lots. No suits, no ties—no dull services.

Other churches use more traditional marketing to reach their target audiences. To attract the boomer/buster set and their kids, the Mormon Church advertises family solidarity and touts the message that spirituality and family are very much tied together.

Has your church studied the demographics of its area? Conducted a market survey? Determined its primary customer base, or activated plans to reach it?

Action: Determine your primary target audience by obtaining demographic information from your city or county and by surveying the congregation. Then make specific plans to reach this target audience.

At a staff or board meeting, talk about your "customers"—what they want, what they expect, what they need, why they come or do not come. Develop a strategy to be more responsive.

The greeter is often the first person in a restaurant or a church to speak to a guest. First impressions set the tone for everything that follows. During those early seconds, a guest gets a feeling of welcome or indifference, a feeling of being glad she came, or wishing she hadn't. Some pointers for churches:

- Greet or acknowledge every guest by name whenever possible.
- Use the guest's name aloud immediately and (when convenient) write it down for follow-up.
- Introduce the person to someone else directly or indirectly either before or after the service.
- Ask the guest what he or she does; it's easier to remember a person if you associate him or her with a job or role.
- Seek out strangers: remember, today's regulars were yesterday's "unknowns."

Do you like being greeted when you enter a restaurant? A church? Some churches have intentionally adopted a policy of anonymity for guests—not singling out anyone for attention or identifying newcomers or visitors. How would that go over in your church? Other churches incorporate a special participatory time during the service to share "joys and concerns" or to recognize guests and celebrate their special occasions (like birthdays and anniversaries). Is that a good idea? Why? Why not?

Action: Discuss at a staff or board meeting your church's present policies about greeting and recognizing people. Decide if anything should be changed. If it should, do it uniformly and consistently.

Visual and sensory cues, from the style of architecture, decor, and colors, to the fixtures, paintings, windows, symbols, acoustics, and the apparel worn by the worship or celebration leaders, should make a statement that complements the mission of your church and makes the target audience feel comfortable and at home.

Does your church convey the concepts you want to portray? Attract those in your target audience? If your church were a restaurant, how would you describe its theme? (Some options: family, gourmet, casual, specialty, cafeteria, coffee shop, ethnic, carry-out, fast-food, drive-in, home-replacement, white tablecloth.)

Action: Replace or change any physical property that detracts, rather than contributes, to the image you want your church to embody.

A mission statement is a written declaration of long-term goals and overall philosophy of an organization—its reason for being. It typically includes a statement of the organization's purpose (end result), the means by which that purpose will be carried out (how you do what you do), and for whom the organization exists (such as customers, the community, staff, God). Mission statements do not include information about daily tactical operations, such as "greet all guests when they walk in the door."

Does your church have a mission statement? How current is it? How clear? Does it include the components listed above?

Action: Develop and implement a mission statement for your church. This can often be done through focus groups that represent the various leadership areas of the church. The governing board and staff then refine and hone this written material into a brief, pithy statement. If you already have a mission statement, use it to test the church's strategies and programs. Do each of them advance your mission? If not, something needs to be changed, dropped, or added.

The menu has been called the restaurant's blueprint. Its many functions include attracting and intriguing customers, providing a guide for ordering, determining the physical layout and special equipment needed, setting the tone (ethnic, formal, etc.), and defining how the facility will be furnished and decorated. Ray Petteruto, in his book *How to Open and Operate a Restaurant*, says the menu is "your image, your face, your personality."

For menu-making, restaurant managers are counseled to consider only possibilities compatible with the restaurant's mission statement. Diversification, just for the sake of having lots of menu items, isn't justified; specialization is usually the key to success. Restaurateurs are also instructed to limit their menu to items for which there is adequate trained staff and equipment so they can be properly prepared and served.

That is true for the Christian church as well. The menu is the church's worship, witness, and work. In essence, it's how the church embodies the Word of God. It's what enables the church's mission. And a bulletin, an order of service, a newsletter, a welcoming booklet can all be the means to present your menu.

But these means of communication should be limited to what will build a reputation for excellence and integrity. Trim the fat and eliminate the mediocre. For example, if you distribute a twenty-page welcoming directory describing your church's activities, better be sure the guests can actually order what's listed there!

How do you present your church "menu"? How appetizing is this menu? Do people read it? Does it attract and intrigue? Does it assist guests to decide what part of the church's worship, word, witness, and work they will take part in? Are there enough choices? Too many?

Action: Study the various publications of your church and take steps to make each one truly reflect your mission. Streamline or redesign your menu, adding or deleting as necessary. Make sure you can deliver what you pledge, that what your guests see is what they get.

CHAPTER 2

Take a Walk to the Village Wok
(Minneapolis, Minnesota)

Wanting to save airfare, I had taken a flight out of Santa Barbara a day early and spent Saturday night in Minneapolis. I awoke to a bright and sunny October Sunday at the Radisson Metrodome Hotel and had the whole day to myself.

After visiting a church and taking a long walk around the nearby University of Minnesota campus, I returned to my hotel room, read the newspaper, and began to think about something to eat. Looking out my window, I discovered at least three small restaurants in the block directly across the street. Only one seemed busy. And it was *very* busy, so I decided to check it out.

The Village Wok on Washington Avenue is a very small ethnic food place, a storefront business, really, takeout and dine-in combined. The location is nothing great. Several deli shops and a coffee house are within several doors, but the Wok is clearly the cafe of choice, both for university students and local Asians, as well as for a general Minneapolis clientele. Some travel considerable distances to eat there. Word of mouth has spread the news that food at the Village Wok is worth standing in line for.

On the Sunday afternoon I was there, the doorway and sidewalk were jammed with patrons waiting for one of the ten or twelve tables inside, or to pick up preordered food. The atmosphere inside the Village Wok is best described as cozy—make that crowded. Once you're seated, you just seem to melt into the ambiance. Perhaps that feeling of being at one with your surroundings is part of the Wok's Asian aura.

It's obvious what food is available on any given day—the handwriting is on the wall. The menu, that is. It's written on large sheets of newsprint or butcher paper and taped up like banners along all four sides of the dining room. The writing is in at least one Asian language, with an English translation below. You have to turn your head and shift your eyes as you look around the room from wall to wall to read the full bill of fare. Nothing is repeated, and there are no printed menus. I think one attractive young lady thought I was staring at her; in reality I was trying to decipher the beef and pea pod entry on the newsprint behind her head.

The fare is Pan-Asian with plenty of variety; the servers and owner are bilingual, maybe trilingual. You feel this is an authentic ethnic restaurant, not a fast-food knockoff where frozen everything is microwaved to death and slapped on your plate.

The food is spicy and piping hot, prepared with fresh ingredients and cooked with an Oriental flourish. Prices are modest to moderate. "Here," I thought to myself as I opened my fortune cookie at the end of a sumptuous meal of beef and pea pods, "not only are you fed, you also get your future destiny revealed!"

If you're looking for quiet and relaxed atmosphere, you may prefer to order the Wok's food to go and eat it at home or in your hotel room; the Wok offers plenty of take-home value.

But if it's a leisurely anniversary date or other special occasion you're celebrating, perhaps you'll walk on by the Wok and places like it. And choose the elegant and expensive—which we'll visit next.

❖

A restaurant or a church doesn't have to be megasize in order to be successful. Sometimes the smaller places are busiest. Guests will drive a long distance to them, then stand in line and wait to be seated in a crowded room with other people who have done the same thing. They have anticipated savory food, are confident the service will be competent and exemplary, and feel secure because they count on quality and consistency in a place stamped with peer approval. In such places there is excitement, a mood of expectancy—the happy hum of conversation in the air that adds to the pleasure. Even if it's only a few tables or a small social hall.

But there need to be sufficient customers or guests. Church leaders sometimes forget that the faithful in the flock as well as the "unchurched" out in the community *have the choice to accept or reject* their menu and their services. They can say no—choose to stay away or go somewhere else. Just because you have "built it" doesn't necessarily mean they will come, to state conversely the axiom made popular by the movie *Field of Dreams*. They must have a *reason* to come and *choose* to come. They need to say yes.

Jim Sullivan, president of Pencom, a Denver hospitality training company, tells managers that the most expensive thing in their operation is an empty chair. In church, an empty seat or pew is the saddest thing: It could be filled by someone who is receiving a benefit, who is being blessed by attending and participating. But to think of the church primarily as the dispenser of what its leaders think the guests need is to misunderstand the church's mission.

First of all, in order to come, that guest must value your service. And he or she must be satisfied in order to keep coming. As management expert Peter Drucker points out in his self-assessment material for nonprofit organizations, "All our customers must want what we deliver."

Is there a happy buzz of excitement in your church? Anticipation? Confidence? What is the primary emphasis—what the pastor or leaders think people ought to do? Or is it creating an environment where the guests find value and satisfaction? How would your church be different if you shifted the focus? Would its people not only be satisfied or fulfilled but also changed?

Action: Survey members of your church to find out what their needs are and what kind of menu would really excite them. Then, if the results fit your mission, serve up those entrees.

Restaurants can get *too* busy. Like when they're overwhelmed with the workload: too many customers and too few workers. People in the business call it "off in the weeds," or "being swamped," or "spending more time in the weeds than an Everglades alligator."

You know what happens in a restaurant when the waiters are in the weeds; the same things happen in church when pastors and the staff feel like that. Poor service. Poor servants!

Are you "in the weeds" at your church? Why? Is it because you're at capacity and maxed out with guests and a full menu? Or are there still lots of empty seats and unfilled jobs? If the former is true, then you need more staff or a bigger building or campus; if the latter, then the problem is inefficient staffing, lack of training, or failing to enable the laity to find their gifts and equip them for ministry.

Action: As a staff or board, get out the Weedeater® and the Round-up®. Plan an attack and clear out the weeds. But remember, they tend to grow back quickly, so try a little preventive maintenance, too.

Customers sometimes tell a waiter that they love the food but just can't stomach the restaurant. They will, however, settle for take-out. When that happens in church—when people won't sit through a worship service that isn't their style or stay for the adult education class—send them home with books and tapes.

CHAPTER 3

Celebration!

L'Auberge (Sedona, Arizona), Chez Panisse (Berkeley, California), and The Ritz-Carlton (Tysons Corner, Virginia)

A double celebration: Our close friends Tom and Starr Harrison were celebrating their anniversary, which falls just four days after Starr's April 1 birthday. This called for something special!

The dining spot had long been decided. And a seven o'clock reservation was made well ahead during our after-Easter getaway trip to Sedona, the red rock mecca of tourism and New Age enlightenment in central Arizona. The unanimous choice was L'Auberge, a fine French restaurant on the left bank of scenic Oak Creek.

Happily seated at our requested creekside table, we found to our pleasure that the window above had been opened slightly so we could hear the tumbling water; in truth, at L'Auberge it seems that the river runs through it.

We felt so special here. The steward poured our wine. We toasted, and Tom and Starr held hands. We didn't notice the clock and were in no hurry to order. Eternity transfixed the now, and I thought of the words of "Like a River Glorious," the Gospel hymn: "not a blast of hurry, not a shade of care, touch the spirit there."

Several hours later Tom and I placed our plastic on the little tray the server had deposited. The price for our wine, appetizer, elegant dinners, and dessert? Value for service and provisions rendered is measured in different ways at different times and occasions. If you need to ask, you shouldn't go to L'Auberge.

Subtle but Simple

It's not the burbling sound of water running through a tranquil Arizona canyon resort you hear at Chez Panisse. At this French restaurant on Shattuck Avenue in Berkeley, California, you may hear the sounds of the bustling campus and business community surrounding it. But a distinctive kind of ambiance pleases as you walk up the narrow stairs at the front of the long, natural wood building that exudes the essence of old-time Berkeley.

It certainly wasn't the inconspicuous wooden sign out front that attracted our attention; we drove by twice before we realized which building was the restaurant. Most patrons, like us, learn about Chez Panisse through those who pass along its outstanding word-of-mouth reputation.

Yes, reservations are accepted—for the downstairs only, where there are a mere sixteen tables. But no earlier than thirty days ahead of the requested date (and never for Fridays or Saturdays). The reserved tables fill fast, so call precisely no sooner or later than thirty days ahead. Otherwise, expect to wait at least an hour during prime evening hours. Dinners up to $100 (with tax and gratuity) are typical, although Monday night prix fixe dinners go for $35.

Upstairs, reservations are accepted for lunch, but only if you make them on the morning of the day you plan to come (not before). The upstairs fare is still sumptuous but the tab is affordable midrange.

Surprisingly, perhaps, this is a place for children as well as for adults (if their parents are well-heeled). Chef Alice Waters, who is also an owner of Chez, invites the five- to ten-year-old set to venture behind the counter to make their own pizza with her or one of the other chefs. Thus, Chez chefs have become teachers. Chez has also published a food book for children.

The Alsatian dinners exemplify the philosophy (I might even say, theology), that Alice has proselytized throughout the country. That, says Patricia Unterman in a review from *The San Francisco Chronicle*, is to "find the best and most seasonal, healthfully raised ingredients—and if they aren't available, raise them yourself; prepare them in ways that reveal their flavors rather than mask them; and always present them beautifully, if simply."

In fact, as ML and I learned from our server as we savored some salad greens from the Chez Panisse gardens, the restaurant contracts with an organic produce farm in Sonoma to exclusively produce its specialty vegetables and salad items.

As we drove down Shattuck Avenue toward the UC Berkeley campus, I thought about Chez's secret of success, which might be emulated by well-run churches of the late 1990s: Every detail is well thought out and carefully planned, but with a simple and subtle style.

I found myself in agreement with restaurant critic Unterman that the experience of eating at Chez Panisse "is so unique and subtle that first-timers have to think about it to get it. Dining there is not the formal or showy experience that people expect from such a famous restaurant. However, you will find that whatever the restaurant decides to put on your table that day, from bread to coffee, will be the best you can find any place in the world."

That's a tasty mouthful of high praise!

Dining at the Ritz

We probably would not have eaten at The Restaurant in the Ritz-Carlton Hotel, except that I was attending a religion and media conference at the Ritz in Tysons Corner, Virginia, and ML was with me to do interviews for *After Your Child Divorces*, her book to help parents rebuild family bonds.

The food was first-class, and so was the service. Elegant and extravagant summed it up, as expected. But something that struck me was the Ritz's emphasis on two weekly events—"two culinary extravaganzas," the flyer called them. They are the Sunday brunch and the Friday night seafood buffet—"two lavish buffets guaranteed to please the most discriminating palate. All the tempting desserts are also available for purchase to serve at your next dinner party."

The Ritz-Carlton is on to a truth about human habits: people will turn out for special events that are held regularly. And, when they like something, they want more of it. Not only will they come back, they will take some home and share it with their family and friends. There is spiritual truth here as well, it dawned on me as I savored fresh fruit sorbet in an orange tuile coupe. I sipped it slowly through the chocolate straw as ML sampled the mango mousse and coconut sorbet with passion fruit sauce.

Another surprise at the Ritz, as there had been at Chez Panisse, was the realization that upscale restaurants often focus on children as well as adult guests. Elegance is not only for adults. At the Tysons Corner Ritz-Carlton, for example, teas are regularly scheduled on Saturday mornings from 11:00 to 12:30. Children and their favorite stuffed animals gather at the Lobby Lounge's cozy fireplace for "Teddy Bear Tea." The event includes sing-alongs with Goldilocks and the Ritz's giant bear. The "beary" tasty menu features hot chocolate, peanut butter, and "beary" sandwiches, teddy bear cut-out cookies, and chocolate bears. At the conclusion of the festivity, each young guest receives a photograph and a Ritz-Carlton gift.

Sorta like a Sunday school picnic? Maybe, but adults pay $18 (plus tax and tip), and children, $15. Teddys are free.

❖

Restaurants USA, the magazine of the National Restaurant Association, says that "consumers perceive restaurants as an oasis, a place where they can have fun with friends and family in a safe setting as well as connect with their community at large." That, it seems to me, is also a pretty fair description of a seeker-sensitive church. Having fun sounds a little frivolous, perhaps—but shouldn't we *enjoy* church? Like the psalmist of old, going into the house of the Lord should make me glad!

Dining out at a fancy or distinctive place is an occasion we often reserve for celebrations—anniversaries, birthdays, graduations, and the like. Couldn't churches emphasize these celebrations, too, with special events? For example, a day each month when couples who are observing their anniversaries could renew their marriage vows in church; baptismal anniversary celebrations; birthday "milestones"; graduation parties.

Some celebrations, like these, are uniquely meaningful to the individual or family; other observances fit generic holiday and calendar events. And some are created. The McCormick & Schmick's restaurants feature a lobster and crab night on Mondays in March and live jazz and blues on Fridays. In Washington, D.C., a downtown shushi bar ties a special meal promotion to the city's annual spring Cherry Blossom Festival. And in Chicago, The Retreat Restaurant shines the spotlight on traditional African cooking every Sunday in February—Black History Month. If restaurants can link their operations with high-profile civic and charity events—emphasizing their solidarity with the community in the process—why can't churches?

What special events does your church observe or promote for individuals, couples, or families? What about community-wide, charitable, or seasonal events? Would observing these events add relevance to your ministry and reach people who would not respond to traditional church activities?

Action: Plan at least one special church event that will tie in with celebrations in the lives of your members, and another one that relates to a holiday, the mission of a local charitable group, or a citywide event.

Culled from the words of restaurant experts:
"Comfortable customers come back . . . with their friends."
"The function of a restaurant and its management is simply this: to make people feel better when they leave than when they arrived."

Is it the job of the church to make people feel comfortable, or uncomfortable? About what? If they are made to feel uncomfortable, will they come back? If they don't return, then what? Is "feel good" theology dangerous? Is there a place for it? Is there a difference between feeling comfortable and being comforted?

Another management maxim is that restaurants should provide hospitality: *"a warm feeling resulting from feeding both the body and the soul."*

Does this quote blend better with the role of the church? Why? What did Jesus say?

Atmosphere is composed of a variety of ingredients—setting, architecture, color, design, sound, temperature, music, etc.—and certainly the *esprit de corps* of the staff.

How valuable would you rate the atmosphere in a restaurant? A church? Do you think it is as important as good "food" and good "service"?

Peter Drucker, in his book *The Five Most Important Questions You Will Ever Ask about Your Nonprofit Organization*, says one of the questions, "What does the customer consider value?" may be the most important, yet least asked. Value may be defined as quality or price, he says, but more importantly, it means that what you are doing is being used. "You must keep in mind that the customer never buys a product. By definition, the customer buys the satisfaction of a want," Drucker says.

Value seems to have a "floating decimal": What is value for a particular occasion—a special anniversary dinner, a wedding party, a funeral service for a loved one—depends on the value assigned by those making the choice. The six-course dinner in the posh restaurant may be of value for one's twenty-fifth wedding anniversary celebration, but not for an ordinary Saturday night out, when Pizza Hut may do just fine.

In the church we often make assumptions about what is of value to our guests based on our own interpretations of their needs. Do we also understand their needs in terms of their own realities and perspectives?

Action: Devise a plan to gather information about what people in your church consider to be of value—what they would "stand in line for"—and under what circumstances. Remember, the guests always make the final decisions: They can come or not come. You may have the best program in the world, but if it isn't perceived as value, it won't be well attended or successful. Factor the results of your study into the church's short- and long-range agendas.

When it comes to choosing a restaurant they haven't tried before, the overwhelming majority of diners rely on word of mouth. According to a restaurant association survey, 86 percent reported they are likely to use a recommendation from a family member, and 85 percent said they'd rely on a recommendation from a friend. Surveys of churchgoers reveal the same thing: Word of mouth is the most potent selection factor for visiting a church.

Does your church have a good word-of-mouth reputation? Or are people saying much of anything? How can you "talk it up" and get the buzz of excitement going through the grapevine and into the community?

Action: Make a plan to spread the word—if you deliver what you're talking.

Some churches include a children's sermon, or a "time up front" for children during the worship service. Other churches eschew the practice as being a distraction, too time-consuming, or of little benefit to the children. When done well, I believe the children's message can be a highlight of the service. It's best if it's interactive—the more participatory and visual, the better. This can be an educational as well as entertaining moment. Skillfully executed, the children's theme can be integrated with the thrust and message of the whole hour, and even advance it. Never think for a moment that the adults aren't taking in every word! (In fact, they may remember it far longer than the three points of the adult sermon.)

Does your church have a time for children to come up front during the service? How well is that time thought out and carried out?

Action: At a meeting of the preaching, worship, and Christian education staff or committee members, review your church's policies about regular children's messages. Either start an excellent one, drop the existing one (if it's poorly done or irrelevant), or upgrade it to a five-star rating.

CHAPTER 4

What's in a Name?

The Impeccable Pig (Scottsdale, Arizona), and The Hard Rock Cafe (Manhattan, New York)

What's in a name? Why do restaurants and churches have the names they do?

Some names denote the family ownership or the chef, like Evan's Farm Inn; Wolfgang Puck Café; First Methodist; First Church of Christ, Scientist. Other names denote the place or locale: Green Street East; Twin Palms Café; Hollywood Presbyterian; Twin Pines Christian. Some names tell you what kind of food you'll find at that place, like the Olive Garden; Red Lobster; Conservative Independent Baptist; Deliverance Chapel. Some are a combination: Chicago Chop House; Sam & Harry's Steak & Ale Emporium; Church of God, Cleveland, Tennessee; Texas Churches of Christ, noninstrumental. Some names connote a mood or ambiance: T.G.I. Friday's; Cracker Barrel Old Country Store; Joybells Fellowship; Haven of Peaceful Rest. Some names just seem to "happen"; others show the owners' carefully thought-out intention to make a statement, sometimes as the result of expensive advertising surveys and marketing research.

Two of my favorite names say something about the establishments they represent: The Impeccable Pig and the Hard Rock Cafes.

The Impeccable Pig, just south of Scottsdale's oldtown on East Indian School Road, was founded in 1978 more as an antique store than as a restaurant. The name immediately suggests an apparent contradiction, or oxymoron: I've never seen a pig that's impeccable—not even close. Never mind, the restaurant/store's logo is a porker attired in bow tie, top hat, and spats. He holds a cravat in his right forepaw as he sedately promenades along on his hind feet. Impeccable, indeed!

Featuring "antiques, cuisine, and a boutique," the Impeccable Pig conveys an elegant farm and country motif through its use of pigs, pheasants, ducks, and cows in paintings, sculptures, and other *objets d'art*—most of which are for sale.

You don't forget the Impeccable Pig. The menu is handwritten on a giant board that is propped on a stand in front of your table. Selections are changed daily to create surprise and interest. This element is often lacking in humdrum, "business as usual" restaurant chains as well as in churches, I concluded as I ordered an Autumn Tortellini, a squash-filled pasta with broccoli cream sauce.

It was early November and cool nights had come to Arizona, so a hearty meat entrée also sounded good. All meat entrées are cooked over an open grill where diners can watch the chef's artistry. I chose the "Unblemished Lamb." I have always liked symbolism.

Hard Rock: Hard Place to Forget

It's 1 A.M. on a Friday, Eric Clapton's guitar is on the wall, the music is blasting, and kids are standing in line a block long waiting to get into Manhattan's Hard Rock Cafe. "Is this any way to run a restaurant?" asks *Forbes* magazine writer Jeffrey A. Trachtenberg.

Apparently it is. The Hard Rocks pack 'em in when trendy, hip restaurants can come and go in a season. The secret? Partly it's smart marketing. And the right name. Hard Rock Cafes are a place between rock and a cafe that people find hard to forget. Especially when you see the initiated wearing Hard Rock T-shirts all over the world.

The Manhattan Hard Rock on West 57th Street features a bar forty feet long and shaped like a Fender Stratocaster guitar. And there's memorabilia that's sacred to the in-crowd: a hat that Jimi Hendrix wore; Jerry Lee Lewis' shoes; fancy guitars played by Clapton, George Harrison, and Pete Townsend, and a drum pounded into immortality by the Beatle's Ringo Starr.

Hard Rock Cafes are living museums. Here, history and popular culture are brought to life around the central human act of consuming food. Who says dining can't be an educational experience? The Hard Rock Cafe is the place for a targeted international clientele to see and be seen in the midst of music, mood, memorabilia, and a meal, and then move on with a T-shirt status trophy.

Hard Rock cofounder Isaac Tigrett said it cost $3.6 million just to open the doors at the Manhattan cafe. But once through them, patrons don't stay long. Hard Rock sound systems, blaring the fast-paced music that is the cafes' signature, are purposely turned up full blast to speed guests on their way. They eat so fast they're gone in an average of about twenty-five minutes, according to one source. They "tap their feet and leave," observed writer Trachtenberg, noting that the 240-seat Manhattan Hard Rock was serving about 2,200 meals between 11:30 A.M. and 4 A.M.

Some successful restaurants and churches are just too noisy for me. I hate it when I can't hear what the person across the table is saying, or I have to shout to make others half hear me. Or, in church, I can't get beyond the beat to the worship, or the shouting gets in the way of the message. When the music is raucous, the food seems secondary to the experience—just "hanging in" at the right place—or else the music is the real draw, not the food. But maybe my attitude about music in restaurants and churches is a reflection of my age. If it's a choice between a Hard Rock or a soft-music place, I guess you know where I stand (or sit).

In any case, the right name is only the beginning. "Your restaurant," declared Hard Rock partner Tigrett, "stays hot as long as people hear about it, but they won't come back if the food isn't any good."

A church can be as solid as the Rock, too, but only as long as the spiritual food is good. If it is prepared well and seasoned delightfully, folks may wait two hours to get a seat.

If you are starting a brand new church, you have the good fortune to be able to choose its name rather than inheriting what may be a prosaic and uninspiring one, like First Avenue United Methodist Church of Anytown. On the other hand, if consensus is needed, it may take weeks or months before a name is agreed on.

Several pointers: (1) Make the name fit the "menu": If it is community-wide appeal you're after, reflect that—"Santa Ynez Valley Church." Scriptural teaching? How about "Neighborhood Bible Church." (2) The name should appeal to the kind of guests comprising your target market. Want to appeal to busters and boomers? Then perhaps eliminate the word "Church," which has old-fashioned or negative connotations to some. Instead, make it "Fellowship" or "Chapel."

A long, formal name tends to get shortened or nicknamed: Everyone calls the First Presbyterian Church of Hollywood "Hollywood Pres." First Presbyterian Church of Columbia, California, an historic church in a restored gold rush town, is known as the "Church of the '49ers." Arlington Temple United Methodist Church is breezily referred to as "Our Lady of Exxon" because it's above the oil company office and gas station in Rosslyn, Virginia.

Should you emphasize—or at least include—the denomination in your church's name? In many minds, denominational identity has become a liability rather than an asset. Saddleback Valley Community Church in Southern California is affiliated with the Southern Baptist Church, but Pastor Rick Warren downplays the tie. Younger generations particularly tend to think of denominations as institutional baggage. These "believers but not belongers" are put off by bureaucracy, seeing it as uncaring and irrelevant.

On the other hand, a church may be proud of its heritage and want to capitalize on the denominational connection and its strengths.

If you are involved in church planting, how much time has been spent studying name options for your fellowship? What criteria are used? If your church belongs to a denomination, how do your guests perceive that identity—positively or negatively? Is there some way to accent the strengths of the affiliation while you also stress the local and independent character of your parish or congregation?

Action: Consider your church's name in light of your mission statement. If the two are in major conflict, obtain the required paperwork and approval to change the name. Review also the names of the organizations, classes, and departments in your church. Change any that don't signal the message you want to send.

If the food is consistently good in a restaurant, a blackboard-type menu may work well: It adds spontaneity to the dining experience and allows people to develop confidence in the chef, rather than in a set, printed menu. The same case is often made for "freestyle," or nonliturgical, churches where there is no formal printed order of service: There is more opportunity for the Holy Spirit to lead the worship, the reasoning goes, and those in charge can better respond to the needs and moods of the people moment by moment. They can sing songs of their choice, and pray and preach when and how "the Spirit moves."

Do you find it unsettling or confusing to be in a worship situation where there is no printed order of service or you don't know what's going to happen next? Or is it a refreshing, liberating experience? Is "freestyle" worship the same as "unplanned" worship? Can a lack of guidelines be a copout for lack of preparation? If a prescribed liturgy is always used, can that be a copout, too? Is there a place for both styles in your church? Would more guests come?

Action: Have the pastoral staff meet with the worship team or worship committee and work through each aspect of the worship or celebration experiences in your church. If you can, agree on at least one change or different approach you'll try.

Consider Calvary Chapel, where the Monday-night Bible study almost defies belief: two thousand young people pack the Costa Mesa facility to hear Christian rock music and an hour-long biblical sermon. The atmosphere, as they say, is "way casual." The beat is hard rock. Dress is funky. And hairstyles range from buzz cuts to spiked to shoulder-length. "It's just cool," exalts 25-year-old Steve, giving a double thumbs-up sign.

"You have to minister to your culture," say the ministers of the laid-back new devout.

Do you agree? If so, are there limits? Can evangelism and trendiness mix? Can you build tomorrow's ministry plans on yesterday's ministry models? Will today's ministry model fossilize into rigid structures in another generation or two?

Christian music—in its multiple 1990s forms—is increasingly

becoming the single greatest positioning factor in defining a congregation's makeup. "Tell me your style of music," says Saddleback's Rick Warren, "and I'll tell you who you are reaching. And I'll tell you who you'll *never* reach." Drums in the sanctuary may do more than split eardrums; they can split churches! Indeed, we are becoming more segregated in church services over styles of music and worship than we are by diversity of race or economic or cultural backgrounds—although these factors may partly determine the music of choice for particular churchgoers or congregations.

Why is this division so pronounced? Why do so many people either intensely like or dislike contemporary and gospel music, or—on the other hand—traditional church music and hymnody?

Many churches are either unaware of or choose to ignore these deeply held musical preferences. And those churches that do orchestrate their music to reach a certain age group often have trouble appealing to those on either side of that spectrum. Thus it's not surprising that many of the fastest-growing megachurches find contemporary Christian music to be the most pleasing to the ears of their primary target audience—folks in their twenties, thirties, and forties.

Is one style of Christian music better than the others or more "spiritual"? Is there a need to be multimusical as well as multicultural in our approach to worship and praise? Is it likely that, in God's tempo, the next generation will rediscover traditional Christian music? Musically, what is a congregation to do that either already has an even distribution of adults from the twenty-somethings to the eighty-pluses or wants to appeal to a wider age range?

Fortunately, Christian music style encompasses a broad spectrum. Although the growing contemporary and gospel genre appears to be the score of the future, there should also be a place for more traditional music, even if that means a church has to creatively adapt one or more of its services to fit this style. And if your church is stuck in the traditional register, it's time to strike a new note as well.

Action: Learn how to sing in parts, and pray for harmony.

CHAPTER 5

Back to the Basics

*The Hitching Post (Buellton, California), Hobee's (Northern California),
and Taco Bell (everywhere)*

Although there's no lack of restaurants in the Santa Ynez Valley north
of Santa Barbara where ML and I spend much of our time, one in particular nearly always gets our nod when we take out-of-town guests to
dinner. That's because the Hitching Post, a roadside steakhouse off
Highway 101 on Route 246 in Buellton, is dependable. We know that,
without fail, the food and service will be excellent, and we and our
guests will leave contented and full.

There's nothing fancy, mind you, about the HP, as the locals call it.
Just the right basic stuff, done to perfection. And it's served up in a
rough-hewn brown building with a plainspoken brown sign: "World's
Best BBQ Steaks."

If it's been raining, the gravel parking lot at the HP is apt to puddle
and be muddy. For a moment, the thought crosses our minds that maybe
this isn't the best place to take out-of-town company after all. But as
soon as we open the car door, we catch the rich scent of oak wood-smoke
and all doubt vanishes. Even before you step inside the HP, you know
that chef/owner Frank Ostini is working his magic at the grill.

The HP decor is starkly simple. The foyer is papered with photos of
old cowpokes and Polaroid shots of guests taken at birthday and anniversary parties. Look hard, and you may recognize a friend or neighbor.
Or one of the rich and famous with Hollywood or horse-farm connec-
tions who frequent these rural parts.

Look toward the kitchen, and the burly man with a mustache you
see in a safari hat and white chef's jacket is Ostini himself, stoking the
iron grill, basting monster slabs of steak with his special oil and vinegar
sauce, and turning artichokes slowly grilling on the back row.

The menu has a good selection, including baby-back pork ribs, grilled fish, and chicken. But it's three to one you'll choose a steak. The basic decision is only which of the three sizes can you handle. "You got a beef?" I ask my friend after he has ordered. "Well, I got a beef, too," I reply, punning: "A perfect steak and a big baked potato."

The meat is Midwestern corn-fed beef, and except for the filet, all are certified Angus. "Good, simple food like this," wrote S. Irene Virbila in *The Los Angeles Times Magazine*, "made with quality ingredients and with care and attention, is becoming harder and harder to find." That's why we keep coming back to the basics at the HP.

Hobee's Has It

If you're on the road in northern California in the Oakland/Palo Alto/ San Jose area, do yourself (and your family) a favor: stop in at one of the Hobee's restaurants. They serve breakfast (all day), lunch, and dinner, but the greatest of these is brunch.

Pretty basic: The BDBIT (The Best Darn Breakfast in Town) is two fresh eggs any style, and country-style hashbrowns served with blueberry coffeecake or toast, for $3.95. Now, a lot of eateries can bring you that, but Hobee's is the only one I know of that does it with such freshness, attentive service, and style. "Indeed," I muse as I watch our server top off my mug of Hobee's hot cinnamon-orange tea for the umpteenth time, "this quality and attention is something many people like, not only at mealtime, but also at churchtime."

Dinner at Hobee's is pretty basic, too, but with a difference. Hobee-made soups (check the blackboard for daily specials) are made fresh daily. There are only six dinner entrées, but they are reliably fresh—and never overcooked. And they are under ten dollars, including a trip to the soup or salad bar.

Healthy foods are a staple on Hobee's menus, too, like Tofu Scramble, an eggless alternative, and organic tofu-vegetable patty hamburgers. Many Hobee's regulars are both health conscious and taste conscious, and they do not want to be deprived of one for the benefit of the other.

People often stand in line in Hobee's gift shop, waiting to be seated for a meal they expect to long remember. Just in case there's any chance of forgetting, they can do as we did: purchase a take-home reminder, such as a package of that delicious cinnamon-orange tea or a Hobee's T-shirt or mug.

Ring That Taco Bell

Sometimes it's said that the big restaurant chains are too unwieldy and slow-moving to change their menus, styles, or approaches, especially in time to meet the changing appetites of consumers of the 1990s who are more demanding and less brand-loyal than those in previous times. Not so. Many restaurants *do* adapt. Those that don't won't last. And I think that's also true for churches.

Imagine McDonald's changing the way it makes hamburgers. Well, it did, reworking its bun recipe in mid-1995.

Imagine Taco Bell, with nearly twenty thousand outlets, rolling out a whole new line of reduced-fat tacos and burritos. Would you believe a new eight-item menu of entrees called Border Lights?

Taco Bell, a unit of PepsiCo until a spinoff in late 1997, was once a fast-food leader with its "value menu." But, sensing that the competition was closing the gap and that there was a trend toward lighter fare and health-conscious customers, Taco Bell brought out Border Lights in the spring of 1995. This campaign to develop a tasty, reduced-fat meal was a bold step, given the fact that most fast-food aficionados aren't particularly looking for "healthy food." Taco Bell's core customer is a 14- to 34-year-old male—ordinarily not the type to fret over fat.

Projections, at least, pumped up PepsiCo's effort—one of the most prominent in the fast-food industry's attempts in the 1990s to market healthier foods. But surprise! Taco Bell officials soon learned that projections alone don't light fuses with customers. Border Lights fizzled, showing that people don't patronize fast-food restaurants to count calories. The lesson for Taco Bell was to stick to its basics—that its basic customers don't care about being fat-free.

Sensing an untapped segment out there that could be reached, recognizing a market or audience hungry for basic values, and then adjusting quickly when the lean stuff needed beefing up: that seems to be ringing Taco's Bell once again.

Concentrating on basic values without sacrificing quality, taste, or service might ring church bells, too.

❖

I heard about a very liberal church that refuses to speak against hell. Instead, they call hell an alternative lifestyle.

I confess I'm not much for hellfire and brimstone sermons, but that's going too far. In an attempt to be relevant and inoffensive, sometimes we jettison the bedrock basics of God's Word.

When vibrant meaning has stagnated into dull habit, then I applaud reengineering the negotiables and innovating progress. But sometimes the pendulum needs to swing back toward center. Edward Craner, director of programming at CrossWinds Church in Dublin, California, notes that "often in an effort to be progressive and maintain the cutting edge, even such nonnegotiables as accurate biblical translations, the primacy of prayer, and Scripture's final authority have been thrown out. Time has eroded the purpose behind many emblems of the church." Americans hunger for both old and new—the traditional and familiar as well as the new and different. Time to get back to the basics—but with quality and freshness.

Do you consider yours to be a "modern" church? Why? Is the leadership willing to test the relevance and soundness of every "negotiable" in the congregation's life? Are there some staid icons? Are there some significant items, either ceremonial or theological, that have been discarded? Should they be resurrected?

Action: Dust off something basic—a traditional ceremony, symbol, or observance—in your church or ministry that's been abandoned in the name of progress. Reintroduce it, for a limited time at least, but invest it with new life. Revive the original story about its use, and reinterpret its underlying biblical foundation and purpose in contemporary terms. Hint: It could be anything from vestments to banners to Gregorian chants to foot-washing to silent meditation to pictures to stations of the cross to a seder meal—and more. Even teaching about hell.

"It used to be," writes Sylvia Somerville in *Restaurants USA*,

that a restaurateur would create a meal and serve it in an inviting setting at a fair price, and customers would enjoy the dining experience. . . . Now diners want more. They want a peek at the mind and soul behind the dishes. . . . Many customers want to understand the culinary tradition, history, and ingredients that shape a restaurant's pedigree. And sometimes they want to be transported to another place or time.

Call it exhibition, if you will. I think churchgoers also want to know the real man or woman behind the podium or pulpit. They want a glimpse of the mind and soul behind the weekly service or celebration. Pastors are often too remote from their guests—especially in a large parish. The "chefs" need to be more visible, more accessible. They need to let their guests in on what happens behind the scenes—how they prepare a sermon, how a worship or celebration service is planned and practiced, how they get ready to teach a class. Church leaders need to get real and transparent—that's a basic.

Do you consider yours to be a "teaching" church? Why? Does the pastoral staff let the guests in on the "mind and soul" behind the "public" meetings? If you are staff, how accessible are you to your guests? Do you explain the basics—the tradition, history, and ingredients that shape your ministry? If so, how frequently? Are you real and transparent?

At the Sheraton Grande Torrey Pines in La Jolla, California, Chef Jim Coleman operates the "Chef's Hotlines" from 4 P.M. to 7 P.M. Mondays through Fridays. Coleman and his staff are available during this time to callers with "any culinary questions."

Action: Announce a "Pastor's Hotline" with regular hours to answer questions about your church or ministry. At an informal class for anyone who's interested, have the staff give an abbreviated demonstration of a typical week in their professional lives. The pastor should explain how he or she chooses sermon texts and other material. Tell the congregation how they can assist the preparation process and share the ministry tasks.

Advice from Peter Drucker: Focus on the basic things you are competent to do: "Results are achieved by concentration, not by splintering." That gigantic organization, the Salvation Army, focuses on only four or five programs. The important thing, says Drucker, is to "find out what we do well so we can do more of it, and what we do not do well, so we can do none of it."

Are you putting your ministry resources where your results are negligible or zero? For each major program or activity, ask, "If we weren't already doing this, would we start doing it now? Does the focus need changing?" (Consult your mission statement.)

Clarity of concept is one of the most difficult things for any business or ministry to achieve. Says Robert F. Autry, chairman of the four thousand Hardee's and Roy Rogers restaurants: "The trick is to stay true to your roots and tell your story."

Action: Focus your church or ministry on doing a few "root things" extremely well—and tell that story loud and clear.

Today, (a) good service is expected, and (an) excellent service is remembered. Pastoral leadership is the key to excellent service. In the heyday of denominations, churches could ignore human resources and management skills and still grow. Today they can't. But pastors typically receive little or no training in these skills. And they are basic!

Action: Send your pastor and staff to management conferences and courses, and connect them with consultation resources that equip and train for leadership.

Says South Carolina Baptist executive Carlisle Driggers:

- Denominations with the best future will be those whose top priority is to strengthen the churches.
- The primary role of the denomination is not to do the work of the churches for them, *but to assist them to do their own work effectively.*
- The question is not whether a denomination will survive, but whether its people will prepare themselves to be used by God in the future that God is building.

In the business book *Competing for the Future*, authors Gary Hamel and C. K. Prahalad identify reasons why great companies fail. Key reasons include an inability to escape the past and an inability to invent the future.

Are you allowing your present success to determine your future strategy or programs? Is your future effectiveness at risk because of apparent past or present success?

Management expert Ken Blanchard puts it this way: "The thinking that got you to where you are today will not take you to the future."

Action: If you are a denominational leader, ponder the above and spread the word. Your basic survival is at stake!

CHAPTER 6

Ample Ambiance and Hospitality
Cold Spring and Mattei's Taverns (Santa Barbara County, California)

Ever notice when you're traveling the interstate that all the fast-food restaurants seem bunched up at the same exit? If the "golden arches" are there, so is Burger King. And likely, there's a Jack-in-the-Box and a Carl's Jr., too. Denny's and Taco Bell are just across the freeway on the other side. Miss them, and it may be a long haul to the next cluster.

The major food-service chains spend millions and millions each year to find and secure the "right" location. Yet, we all know of restaurants that are successful, seemingly in spite of their location. But think about it a moment. Was that location once a very important and "right" one? Is the restaurant's continued success and large customer volume a result of careful build-up and excellent food and service that keeps customers coming?

Some of these restaurants have achieved what restaurateurs call "destination status." Walt McDowell, my restaurant consultant cousin, explains that designation: The restaurant's existence is the chief reason people go to a particular place. The restaurant is so excellent and unique that people want to "be there." He once managed an eatery in Bodega Bay, a scenic coastal spot an hour or so north of San Francisco. People would make the loop, stopping at the restaurant to eat, and then returning to the city by an inland route. A nice Sunday outing. "You feel like you're extricating yourself from the hubbub," said Walt. "Sometimes the best location is a 'bad' location."

Then there's the Harbor View, a family dining cafe on the bank of the Mississippi River. The Harbor View sits across from a marina at Pepin, Wisconsin, about seventy-five miles from the Twin Cities. There are only eighty seats, and in summer the waits are long: families drive an hour or two and then wait up to two more hours to be served delicious

food. Meanwhile, they enjoy the beautiful ambiance of Lake Pepin and
the friendly rapport; they can even borrow books from a small library
the restaurant maintains. "We're like family here," say the two partner
families who own the Harbor View.

What is it that creates these destination restaurants? Often it's the
ambiance—and the hospitality.

The Cold Spring Relay Station

More than one hundred years ago, dusty stagecoaches filled with hungry
and thirsty passengers stopped at Mattei's Tavern. The site of the original
hotel and restaurant of the 1880s in Los Olivos, California, Mattei's was
the overnight stop on the stage line south to Santa Barbara. And Cold
Spring Tavern, halfway between the two near the top of San Marcos
Pass, was another welcome place of refreshment, nestled in a shady,
dark canyon among huge oaks and pines.

Today, of course, the horse-drawn stages have long since gone. But
travelers come here still, seeking cool refreshment, sturdy sustenance,
and a chance to commune with the rich past of California history. Those
who make the trek over the roads less traveled are rewarded with ample
ambiance and hospitality.

The Cold Spring Tavern, once called the Cold Spring Relay Station,
is arguably California's most rustic inn. It certainly is one of the hardest
to find. On San Marcos Pass (north on Highway 154), you have to be on
the lookout past the crest for Stagecoach Road. Turn left there, follow
the poorly marked road to the right and down the canyon. By and by
you'll see a vine-covered cluster of log-and-shingle buildings. You're
there!

What is now the Log Cabin Bar was once a bottling plant where
Cold Spring's sparkling clear mountain water was bottled and sold as
"the purest water in the county." The small gift shop was the place
where weary stage drivers bedded down for the night. And the trans-
planted jailhouse, obscured by a large fence, was trucked from Ojai
over three mountain passes to its present site under the bay trees.

For me, the tavern dining room holds the most charm. Several side
rooms are very private and cozy, with wood-burning fireplaces and
views of the woods. One room looks out at the cold spring itself and is

a romantic tuck-away setting for an intimate party. The board walls in the dining room are so weather-beaten that ivy tendrils from the outside poke their way through the cracks. Every artifact on the walls bespeaks the Old West—from sepia photographs to barbed wire. If these warped planks could talk, they'd tell of old-time hospitality and the colorful characters who once found solace here. Concord wagons, pulled by four-horse teams, plied passengers, Wells Fargo Express boxes, and the U.S. mail back and forth over the twisting pass. They stopped at the station at noontime for food and drink.

Those yesteryears brought their fill of excitement. Sometimes bandits held up the stage drivers when they were changing teams. Heisting the Wells Fargo box, the thieves absconded up the steep, brushy canyon with the sheriff's posse hot on their heels.

Famous historical figures rode the line in those days. Susan B. Anthony, the controversial suffragette, once arrived at Cold Spring Station, her skirts billowing, as she rode up top with the driver because the coach was full. Today, diners are far removed from these rustic tales of California history, yet they are still strangely fascinated by them.

Cold Spring Tavern has evolved into a prestigious, casual restaurant. Instead of looking out the window as a stagecoach draws up, you may see a long, sleek limousine with darkened windows approaching at sunset, discharging its cargo of the rich and famous from Santa Barbara, or even as far away as Malibu, Beverly Hills, or Hollywood.

Discreetly obscured microwave ovens and unobtrusive computer monitors in the dining room attest to modernity at Cold Spring. And the contemporary cuisine includes sautéed medallions of rabbit, grilled filet of New Zealand venison, and Oh Baby, That's It! (baby-back pork ribs with Cold Spring's own BBQ sauce).

The menu itself is a piquant blend of new and old, modern days and times gone by. As we waited for our New Zealand venison with wild lingonberries, my pastor and his wife and I chuckled over the "Ten Commandments for Stage Passengers" printed on the backside of the menu. A sampling of old stagecoach rules:

7. Firearms may be kept on your person, for use in emergencies. Do not discharge them for pleasure, or shoot at wild animals along the roadside. The noise riles the horses.

9. Topics of discussion to be avoided have to do with religion, politics, and above all, stagecoach robbery or accidents.

Number 10 is my favorite: Gentlemen guilty of unchivalrous behavior toward lady passengers will be put off the stage. It is a long walk back to Santa Barbara. A word to the wise is sufficient.

Mattei's: Another Nineteenth-Century Stagecoach Inn

Travel on down Highway 154 about twenty miles through the Santa Ynez Valley to a point five miles northwest of Solvang: Here, folks are also intrigued with the ambiance of a onetime stage stop called Mattei's Tavern. In 1886, this restaurant opened as the two-story Central Hotel of Los Olivos. But it was the restaurant's widespread reputation for gourmet food that drew travelers to Mattei's.

In buckboard days, celebrities flocked to Mattei's, and they still do. Old guest registers display the signatures of a Vanderbilt, a Rockefeller, and a Lorillard. Later guests include Herbert Hoover, William Jennings Bryan, and an abundance of movie stars—Clark Gable, Gary Cooper, Carole Lombard, Bing Crosby, Marjorie Main, and Rosalind Russell, among others.

On a weekend, you'll probably have to wait a while for a table. So look around the old rustic lounge. Check out the photos and maps from Wild West days. Peruse the portraits and paintings by Clarence Mattei, son of tavern founder Felix Mattei. And if you only have time for dessert, try a mudpie.

Personally, ML and I like to sit by the big fireplace in the main entry room, or kick back out on the sunporch with the high-back wicker chairs and tables. Sometimes, when we're at Mattei's, I reminisce about the home-cooking of Felix's era. Dinner was prepared from fresh vegetables grown in the back garden, fruit was plucked from the family orchard, and trout were reeled in from nearby Alamo Pintado Creek.

Those days are gone forever, but perhaps there's a lesson about history lessons here.

❖

Almost from its beginning, the Christian church was generally the only recognized institution one encountered from one country to the next. The church maintained hospices (a type of inn), monasteries, and other religious houses that were havens for travelers. The Knights of Saint John of Jerusalem, for example, a religious order founded in 1048, established many cathedrals and monasteries to protect pilgrims on their way to and from the sacred city. The church, in effect, operated the first hotel chain. And providing food and hospitality were at the forefront of Christian mission.

The church's rich history needs to be preserved and presented in a manner that is as appealing as Cold Spring and Mattei's Taverns. Ample ambiance can help us recall the times of the Founder, and appreciate the mission that sparked the growth and deepening of the church's original reason for being, all in a setting where guests can celebrate the heritage of the past while relishing the best achievements of the present.

Like the fast-food chains bunched together at freeway exits, churches, too, often seem to congregate along "church row." Only in the past decade have church planters seriously begun to put a premium on easy freeway access, massive off-street parking, and "destination status." (These are sometimes mutually exclusive, by the way.)

Is your church in the "right" location? Is it compatible with its immediate neighborhood? Why or why not? Is that location downtown? Mostly commercial? Industrial? Residential (single-family or high-rise)? College setting? Rural or farm area? Resort? Is the church campus scenic?

How could you best take advantage of the strengths your church or ministry location offers? Could you capitalize on your surroundings, such as natural or manmade attractions, to achieve "destination status"? Is new housing coming in? Recreation centers? Schools? Shopping malls? Offices? Entertainment? Highways? New zoning or parking requirements or restrictions? Do you have enough room to expand? What will the neighborhood be like ten years from now? Twenty? Will those around you now be there then? Will you?

Action: Propose to your decision-making authorities an expanded ministry that enhances your location, such as establishing low-cost housing for senior citizens; an outdoor amphitheater or indoor theater; a retreat or conference center; picnic area and park or campground; RV park; day-care center; school or university; counseling center; radio or television station or studios; soup kitchen or thrift shop; gymnasium or fitness center; playground; satellite telecommunications center.

How about an on-site restaurant!? ("The Food Court" at Willow Creek Community Church in South Barrington, Illinois, and a restaurant in the North Phoenix Baptist Church are two that I'm aware of.)

Or else propose a new location. Prepare to justify the move and a plan to finance it. In any case, your buildings are an advertisement. Tasteful use of lettering and color, outdoor artwork, pleasing architecture, and aesthetic landscaping should send a message congruent with your mission statement to everyone who passes by—and (it is hoped) stops in.

The finance, management, and control aspects of a restaurant or a church need to be in the background, running like a good software program (i.e., Windows or Mac applications). That frees the staff to be attentive to and enjoy the more creative side (what you're working on, on the screen)—like "menu" selection, "cooking," serving, and personal interaction with the guests. This concentration in the background ensures that up front you'll have the resources required for the careful planning and execution of your mission statement—in a pleasing ambiance.

Is your church or ministry staff freed up for ministry because managerial, financial, and administrative tasks are quietly running in the background? Or are staff (and you) bogged down because these tasks are the front-and-center items that keep popping up on your activity "screen" all the time?

Action: At a staff meeting identify the background tasks that need to run smoothly in order to make your time with your "guests" uncluttered and brimming with full attention. Then identify the programs, tools, supplies, resources, and personnel you need to make that happen for the frontline servers. Train the people. And plug them in! But remember, high tech will never replace high touch.

Perhaps taking a cue from the Christian church's traditional commitment to care for its neighbors, a number of restaurants now sponsor community service programs. One of the best known is the Ronald McDonald House charity of the McDonald's chain. Another, McCormick & Schmick's seafood restaurants help local high schools every spring. During the "tally" period, guests write the name of the school they want to support on the back of their receipt and turn it in at the reception desk. The "ballots" are counted and the winning school receives $25,000 from McCormick & Schmick's to use toward a nonalcoholic spring prom or graduation party.

In the Uptown neighborhood on Chicago's north side, the Inspiration Cafe offers the homeless food and respect as well as housing and job counseling. The cafe is a reservations only restaurant; guests are referred by social service agencies and must have a reservation card to be served.

That's far more community involvement than a lot of churches muster!

Action: Steal ideas from these restaurants! After all, who pioneered the idea of helping others and showing hospitality? (Read Luke 10:25-37.)

CHAPTER 7

Ethnic Adaptability
Angelina's (Baltimore, Maryland) and Fazoli's (Winchester, Kentucky)

Angelina's, at 7135 Harford Road, Baltimore, continues to do what it has done best for the past forty-some years: serve up the city's best crab cakes (voted "best crab cakes" for twelve years in a row by *Baltimore Magazine*). In Maryland, where crab cakes are a special tradition, that's no small accomplishment.

I enjoyed the eight-ounce award-winning jumbo lump crab cake dinner the one and only time I've been to Angelina's. It was April 19, 1994—the night my mother died, although I didn't realize it at the time. I had been speaking at a conference for urban Southern Baptist ministers in Baltimore that day, and two of them had taken me out to dinner afterward. News of my mother's death at age eighty-nine did not reach me until I was at the airport the following morning. I learned that my mother's passing occurred at the very time I was eating at Angelina's. My mother, who relished good food well prepared, would have liked Angelina's. I wish we could have been together for her last meal!

This red brick restaurant near the beltway exit at Parkville is memorable to many people because of its adaptability. It has reinvented itself over the years. Let me explain:

Angelina's is "an Italian restaurant with an Irish pub, famous for crab cakes." Italian? Irish? Local Maryland seafood? Yup. All of these.

Angelina's is multiethnic, with a full Italian menu. And a full American menu. But the "Angelina's" sign out front has a shamrock on it, and there is an Irish pub in the basement called the "Shebeen." Here you find Irish drinks, entertainment on Friday evenings, and cable television. Angelina's also does banquets, caters, and ships crab cakes anywhere in the United States overnight.

For details, call Bob Bufano, Carole Reilly, or Bill Barrett—

Italian, Irish, American; take your pick. Ethnicity in spades (or shamrocks). The reason for the hybrid approach is twofold: first, it reflects changes in ownership through the years. The restaurant passed from Italian to Irish to blended ownership. The night I ate at Angelina's, the previous two owners and the present one were *all* there! It is a happy "marriage": ethnic harmony, a spirit of cooperation, and unity in purpose.

And that leads to the second reason for Angelina's variegated approach: dramatic demographic shifts have overtaken Baltimore in recent years. The ethnic makeup of the neighborhood around Angelina's has changed considerably and is still in transition.

But rather than catering to a diminishing crowd, Angelina's has flexed with the times, creating cuisine that appeals broadly, as well as continuing to cater to the specific ethnic groups that have traditionally comprised the restaurant's core clientele. Unlike the Village Wok in Minneapolis, which serves only Asian food, Angelina's is ethnically diverse. Yet all food is cooked to order and prepared on the premises (no fast food).

Fazoli's Italian Food—Fast

Nearly a year after crab cakes at Angelina's, I was eating lunch at Fazoli's in Winchester, Kentucky. The experience evoked another model of ethnic adaptability. At Fazoli's, dining is conclusively and exclusively Italian, from decor to menu to music. It's good. And fast. "Fazoli's, your favorite fast Italian restaurant, is taking the country by storm!" advises a brochure listing the chain's one hundred locations in ten central and southeastern states. "Fazoli's serves up a fleet of favorites from alfredo to ziti, cooked good and slow, but served real fast. And twelve menu items under $3 make for great money mileage. Unlimited freshly baked breadsticks served with all dine-in entrees. Dine in, carry out, or drive through."

So what's so surprising about a successful new Italian restaurant chain? Fazoli's, headquartered in Lexington, Kentucky, is introducing Italian food to a part of the country where the big-time fare traditionally has been ham, grits, greens, burgers, and barbecue. Fazoli's slogan is, "You're a lot closer to Italy than you may think."

In an effort to convince Southeastern clientele that this is true,

Fazoli's distributes little leaflets called "Fazoli's Food Facts." Their purpose is to acquaint the burger-and-fries crowd with Italian food that is both "nutritious and good for you" (perhaps the redundancy is intended to make sure you get the point).

"Lotta folks here don't know what pasta is," said Gene Stefaniak, general manager of the Winchester Fazoli's. The handout informs that pasta is "a nutritious, high-protein, low-fat grain product" and that Fazoli's pasta is made from North Dakota durum wheat, ground into semolina flour. Heartland farmers can relate to that.

Other educational fun food facts at Fazoli's: There are more than one thousand registered pasta shapes in Italy, and Thomas Jefferson introduced pasta to America. So it's real Italian, real American, and real smart to eat Fazoli's pasta.

ML and I enjoyed our healthy, well-balanced Fazoli's pasta. "Do you serve spumoni for dessert?" I asked.

"We tried that for a while," responded manager Stefaniak, "but no one knew what it was and we had to drop it."

But so far, Fazoli's unlimited breadsticks are doing well in the rural Southeast.

Sometimes, you have to work to overcome prejudice against unfamiliar or untried practices or tastes. Maybe Fazoli's is on an Italian mission, pasta-packing ambassador of friendship and fettucini. Experiencing other styles of food, culture, and worship can make for a healthy and balanced diet. And in today's ecumenical climate, perhaps we're a whole lot closer to Italy than we think!

❖

A restaurant management handbook says *cuisine* is "the style or manner in which food is prepared and is usually associated with a specific nationality or region of a country." Recently I clipped a newspaper article that calls American cuisine "a crazy quilt." A large colored map of the United States (in a quilt design) pinpoints typical ethnic foods associated with different regions: pike, perch, and farm trout in the Heartland; steak and potatoes in the West; jicama, cilantro, and beef barbecue in Texas; citrus, grouper, and mangoes in the Florida South Coastal Caribbean. You get the idea.

Is American religion also an ethnic and regional crazy quilt? Yes and no. A good deal of homogenization has taken place. But regional differences are still noticeable. The mix is especially conspicuous in inner cities and urban cores where sweeping demographic and cultural changes have eroded old city neighborhoods—which formerly substituted for small towns.

"The old ties that bind are no longer there," says Lowell Livezey, director of the Religion in America program at the University of Illinois, Chicago. So these urbanites—many of whom are now suburbanites—need churches and parachurch ministries to help them sustain cultural identities and find a sense of community.

It can be done, as churches reinvent themselves. Livezey and his team were surprised to find a high number of vital urban congregations in Chicago's patchwork of neighborhoods despite high population turnovers. One old Roman Catholic parish, for example, had only four remaining parishioners a few years ago. Now it has a robust 1,500 "Catholic yuppies" who used to live in the city and who drive in from the suburbs to the landmark church building to attend weekend liturgies and experience "spiritual belonging" with city-dwellers. Although the ethnic suburbanites no longer live downtown, they still identify with the inner city and its ethnic diversity.

This "drive-in" community is but one example of a congregation adapting to radical restructuring of society. "Geography is no longer destiny," notes Livezey.

As I stuck my head in the Irish Shebeen at Angelina's restaurant, I thought about some of the other churches that have also done well adapting to demographic change. Like Angelina's, they have stood their ground downtown rather than bailing to the suburbs. I thought of "nesting" congregations, where signs in multiple languages above the sanctuary indicate, for example, that a church is home to believers of Asian, Spanish, and Anglo cultures, and of churches where separate services are held in multiple languages for each group. Angelina's also called to mind the time I visited a Russian-speaking Baptist congregation in Sacramento that met on Friday nights in the Chinese Assembly of God Church.

But I have yet to find a church where the past two pastors and the present one are all still preaching to the same congregation.

Wherever survival and growth take place, change is not only recognized, it works to the advantage of ministry and kingdom building.

Three possible styles for multiracial congregations include (1) a "mother" congregation that births and weans "daughter" churches that meet on either the same or different sites; (2) separate but "equal" congregations that are not related, that meet in the same or different buildings on the church campus; and (3) the diverse congregation model, where ethnic and racial diversity are reflected in the "rainbow" composition of the one church.

Does your church reflect cultural, ethnic, or racial diversity? Does this pattern mirror what has been going on in your region or neighborhood? Why or why not? Is change in the composition, flavor, and emphasis of your ministry desirable? A goal? A part of your mission statement?

Action: Form small groups to explore and prepare the way for change in your church or ministry. (Caution: moving from the idea to achievement will take considerable time!) If your ultimate goal is a diverse congregation, perhaps a parallel ministry—where ethnic or language differences are maintained—is the way to go as an interim step. Look for a "transitional generation" in the makeup of your organization to provide leadership and a bridge to the future. (And remember the power of music and worship style—see chapter 4.)

Pencom, the Denver organization that provides resources for hospitality training, sells motivational posters. My favorite has these four lines at the top:

IYAD

WYAD

YAG

WYAG

Underneath is the translation: "If you always do what you always did, you always get what you always got."

Phil Hagans, once a poor, inner city black youth from Houston, applied that principle to his dismal neighborhood. Now the owner of two

McDonald's franchises there, he has become a beacon of hope for countless young people.

A front page *Wall Street Journal* article about Hagans points to the fact that he and other black McDonald's owners make their inner city businesses thrive and at the same time play a crucial role in the life of poor neighborhoods. Hagans and the other entrepreneurs become advisers, counselors, and teachers to kids in these neighborhoods—"the missing link" in their lives. "You become almost a surrogate parent," says Hagans.

He offers them both jobs and a role model—teaching the work ethic, how to dress, the importance of showing up on time, and working as a team. In sum, his creative approach is enabling urban teens to climb out of the grinding generational ruts that trap so many.

Are black-owned fast-food outlets a route to opportunity and stability in the inner city? Yes, and more. In one racially mixed community, Hagans doubled sales by going to churches and day care centers, encouraging people to hold birthday parties and meetings in his restaurant. Later, he did something that *Wall Street Journal* writer Jonathan Kaufman said a white manager might never think of: He hired a gospel group to serenade black churchgoers while they ate their Egg McMuffins on Sunday mornings. One small problem: The breakfast serenading became so popular folks started showing up late for church. (Hagans switched the gospel gigs to Sunday afternoons.)

Hagans offers financial-planning classes for his workers; he counsels those who are slipping into drug use or alcoholism; he goes to local high schools and conducts a kind of boot camp for job-seekers so they can handle applications and job interviews; he pays for books for workers who are enrolled in college; and he plans to set up an equivalency course for employees who dropped out of high school.

Does your youth program include any of this kind of assistance? Could it? Consider other creative ministries for inner city youth, where ethnic adaptability is a prerequisite. What about a reverse twist, taking the Gospel to places where people eat and hang out, as well as persuading them to come to you?

Action: Plan at least one inner city evangelistic outreach that combines Gospel values with practical hands-on help. Involve "minority" leaders in the endeavor, and partner with other churches, ministries, and community agencies where appropriate. But know your partnership boundaries and don't compromise your mission; beliefs (core truth); or viability (ability to function independently). And definitely don't "over-promise" (that's programmed failure)!

Nowadays, many recipes promise meals in twenty minutes compared with thirty minutes a few years ago. Corporate home economists are cutting back the average number of ingredients in a recipe—down to six or fewer from as many as ten. Only two to four preparation steps are permissible. And directions have to be succinct and simple: words like *mix, stir,* and *heat* pass; words like *julienne* don't. The flavors may not be perfect, but many consumers will trade tastiness for a quick fix.

Has fast food come to the church as well? A new thirty-minute "express worship" service at Highland Baptist Church in Louisville has scored big with the laid-back crowd. Fly-by worshippers like casual dress, finishing quickly, and being "outta there" in time to pursue other activities during the rest of the day.

What do you think about "quickie" services? Do they appeal to ethnic-culture inner city residents? To those who work weekend shifts? Is shorter better for some people? What are the dangers?

Action: Consider launching "Express Worship" or "Celebration-on-the-Fly" for the summer months. As an experiment, hold the miniservice on Saturday evenings or early Sunday mornings. Try a little drama and role-playing, as well as singing, prayer, and a punchy sermonette. A crucial test: Do express worship services hurt attendance at your "traditional" services? Are new people being reached? Do these services draw in ethnic groups?

Design a plan to draw the "express lane" folks into deeper discipleship and permanent involvement.

CHAPTER 8

Classy Excellence
The City Hotel (Columbia, California)

In 1856, George Morgan built a two-story redbrick building on Main
Street in Columbia. It was California's gold-mining heyday, and buildings smack in the middle of town were being torn down by fevered
miners anxious to dig the ore-laden soil beneath them. Today, visitors
to the old City Hotel are eager to claim the treasures inside the building
rather than under it.

This choice hostelry is nestled in a state historic park in the city
that once was known as the "gem of the southern mines." Today, the
hotel houses one of the finest restaurants in northern California. The
City Hotel, as it has been called ever since 1874, offers "white-table-
cloth" fine dining in a formal but relaxed setting. The restaurant features
a contemporary approach to classical cuisine in the old-fashioned gold
rush atmosphere of the 1850s and 1860s. Call it Classy Excellence.

In some ways, the ambiance at the City Hotel reminds me of Cold
Spring and Mattei's Taverns to the south in Santa Barbara County.
Similarly, the City Hotel is close to where we live and attend church
when we're in the central Sierra foothills. Go north two and a half miles
past Sonora on Highway 49, then two miles north on Parrotts Ferry Road,
and you'll reach the heart of historic Columbia.

The entire town is managed by the State Parks Department; the
City Hotel is but one of many splendid old frontier buildings that have
been preserved and given a face-lift. The rustic charm and living museum
qualities of Columbia attract tourists by the tens of thousands each year.

The City Hotel's What Cheer Saloon (complete with a brass cash
register resting on the original cherrywood bar) and ten beautiful rooms,
handsomely appointed with select antiques, are a major draw. But the
dining room alone has catapulted the hotel's rising star into a wide orbit

of fame. Yet, the secret of the City Hotel's success is more than food, however delicious, and more than the ambiance, however authentic and intriguing. It's tableside showmanship, special events created to engross guests in a total experience. Most events are sold out months in advance.

There are winemaker dinners, mystery weekends, culinary classes, dinner and theater packages (including a stage play at the famed Fallon House Theater down the street), and the acclaimed Victorian Christmas Feast celebration.

Columbia Miners' Christmas

Picture eighty guests, many dressed in full Victorian costume. As they arrive in the hotel lobby decorated with evergreen boughs, they are escorted to the large parlor at the top of the stairs. Proprietor "George Morgan" announces every guest by name, handing each a glass of Folie a Deux Sparkling Fantasie or a nonalcoholic alternative. As the evening progresses, the hotel and dining room staff plus several professionals from the Fallon House Theater engage the party in a Western drama of heartbreak and suspense. We boo the villain and cheer for the calamity-prone heroine.

The drama continues intermittently as we work our way through smoked salmon and scallop galantine and oysters on the half shell, followed by wild mushroom velouté with herb croutons and truffle oil.

The guests are really into it now. Conversation is animated. The boom days of the mining era are becoming palpably real, course by course. The pepper-seared roasted beef and roasted quail with shallot bourbon sauce help make this meal *very* special.

Yorkshire pudding. Cranberry-cherry chutney. Winter vegetable gratin. We make plans to invite the couple next to us—whom we have just met—to our home during the holidays. Dessert. The heroine is going to escape. The evil desperados will meet justice on the gallows. Hooray! So the chocolate devil's food cake with vanilla crème fraîche filling and chambord anglaise has no real power over us, after all (except maybe an inch or two at the belt line). By the time our host, "George Morgan," and the entire City Hotel staff wish us a Merry Christmas and bid us farewell, we have, indeed, savored a Columbia Miners' Christmas!

As we step out into the crisp December air, it seems the streets of the town are dressed as they might have been a hundred years ago in anticipation of St. Nicholas' arrival by stagecoach. You can almost hear the auctioneer's voice as he auctions the Christmas trees, and the sound of treat-filled piñatas breaking under exuberant youthful blows. Was that a candlelight parade passing in the distance? Campfires glow, chestnuts are roasting, and carolers stroll in top hats and hooped gowns.

It is, as the menu/program for the City Hotel's Victorian Christmas Feast reminds, "a time for children to dream and adults to remember, and peace to fill the hearts of all."

That's a good reminder and goal at Christmastime for church folks as well!

Hospitality Management Training

Another unique aspect of the City Hotel is that it is a training center for students enrolled in hospitality management courses at nearby Columbia Community College. About seven hundred colleges, universities, and private institutions throughout the country offer this course track. The certificate in Culinary Arts at Columbia College takes four semesters. Francis Lynch, who headed the program for years, noted that about seventy students were enrolled in the popular program and "we are running out of room."

The practical, hands-on approach affords budding chefs, maître-d's, restaurateurs, and hospitality managers an opportunity to taste success as they train at the on-campus Cellar Restaurant. And during their final year, they work alongside the professional staff at the elegant City Hotel. Here they not only learn the recipes, memorize the menu, and sample the soup—they wear the authentic clothes of the colorful era that the hotel represents.

"This is a very healthy field right now," says Lynch, dressed in checkered pants, a white jacket with a gold name-badge, and a white linen scarf. While we chat in the Cellar Restaurant he plans a party for two hundred, buying chicken and pearl potatoes from a vendor who taps the order into his laptop computer.

"But I tell students," sighs Lynch, "that the hours are very long."

He also tells them that running a successful restaurant:

- is a very people-oriented operation.

- requires all the skills of leadership.
- requires family skills: "It is running a household for profit."
- requires the ability to be sociable.
- takes happy staff to make happy guests.
- doesn't just happen: "You've got to create it."

Hmm. Sounds like these principles apply to flourishing churches, too. Did my seminary professors ever tell me anything like that?

❖

Experts agree that restaurant is theater. Says Daniel Miller, author of *Starting a Small Restaurant*:

> From the moment the customers first make contact with the players . . . the tone of the response they get is essential to their dining pleasure. As in theater, both the voice and the body must convey your message. The message a small restaurant gives is friendship, calm and graceful service, and artfully prepared food of the highest quality. The mood and demeanor of the dining room staff bespeaks this message in the subtlest ways.

Guests may come for food, but they "want to be entertained, to have an adventure, and to try something new," advises Carol Ann Caprione Chmelynski in *Opportunities in Restaurant Careers*. "Dinner in a restaurant . . . has now become the theater. Dining out has become the show."

Veteran restaurateurs Jim Sullivan and Phil Roberts put it this way:

> We're in *show business* every day. . . . An effective restaurant manager is like the writer, producer, and director. . . . You must audition, rehearse, and cast both the "actors" (front of the house) and the "technicians" (heart of the house). You may have to rewrite the "script" (service and sales focus)—daily—to accommodate the ever-changing elements of the cast, crew, theater, and even the audience.

Is a church or ministry "theater"? Is it "opening night" every time you unlock the front door for a service or event? How important (and adequate) are rehearsals? What are the equivalents of costumes, uniforms, and props? Who are the "actors"? The "technicians"? While a church doesn't exist by ticket sales, it does depend on guests supporting the ministry. If you're playing to a half-empty house, 50 percent of the audience isn't there. How likely is it that that half will give (buy into the ministry) financially?

Is the pastor regularly present, encouraging, and coaching "award-winning" performances from the cast and crew each and every time the curtain goes up? Most importantly, is the divine "Producer-Director" there, daily, in the wings, directing, leading, correcting, and praising?

Action: Organize a small drama group within your church or ministry. Create an original play or skit that compares gospel ministry to dinner theater. Perform the play, either during a worship service or at a special function. Invite reaction during a talkback session following the performance.

Stand-up comedians in church. Laughter in the pews over religious jokes. Is a church any place for this? Isn't it mixing the sacred and the silly? Or maybe even blasphemy? Folks at Bel Air Presbyterian Church in Los Angeles don't think so. This church is but one of a growing number turning their sanctuaries into a venue for comedy that features Christian jesters with squeaky-clean routines.

More serious theater is connected with many large congregations. First Presbyterian Church of Hollywood has an on-site production company and theater. Several times a year Willow Creek Community Church outside of Chicago features quality musical dramas written, produced, and performed by its members. So does Overlake Christian Church in Kirkland, Washington. These are in addition to less formal drama played in these churches at many services.

Interdenominational and independent Christian drama and mime troupes perform in churches and "road shows" across the nation. Often, area fellowships join in sponsoring these groups and events. I recently saw *Heaven's Gates and Hell's Flames*, a play (a glorified skit, really) produced by Reality Outreach of Niagara Falls, New York. An evangelist, props, and skeleton crew are provided, but local talent is recruited and whipped into performance-shape two weeks or less ahead of opening night. *Hell's Flames* is definitely a hard sell, but tens of thousands of those who attend it—including many unchurched teens—respond by committing their lives to Jesus Christ at the closing invitation. I think high-impact drama is the wave of the future for evangelism.

Action: Plan regular musical and dramatic presentations that reach beyond your parish to the broader community. Create special events that engross guests in a total experience.

In chapter 3 we touched briefly on the importance of holidays and seasonal happenings. Here's a list of significant dates to help your planning:

New Year's Day, Presidents' Day, Black History Month, Valentine's Day, Chinese New Year, Washington's Birthday, Ash Wednesday, Lent, St. Patrick's Day, Holy Week, Palm Sunday, Maundy Thursday, Passover, Good Friday, Easter, Ascension Day, Cinco de Mayo, Mother's Day,

Armed Forces Day, Victoria Day (Canada), Memorial Day, Pentecost, Flag Day, Father's Day, Dominion Day (Canada), Independence Day, Labor Day, Columbus Day, Halloween, Election Day, Veteran's Day, Thanksgiving, Advent, Christmas, Epiphany. You can add more.

Such events not only tie in your church or ministry with civic and national pride and identity, they can also appeal to people who are not drawn to traditional Sunday services. Many do respond to special family occasions and to civil and patriotic themes that interest them or evoke significant (and often nostalgic) memories.

Can your church or ministry take advantage of these special dates?

Someone said service is love in work clothes. Sounds easy but it takes work (not just clothes). It also takes training, teamwork, practice, patience, and prayer, just for starters. Service is the main dish we have to offer in today's marketplace and ministry.

One great mistake many restaurants make is having inexperienced employees train new people when they themselves have never been properly trained. Staff—both professional and volunteer—must be properly trained in leadership skills *in the beginning*.

That's why hands-on supervised training is the key to excellence in leadership and service. Classroom lectures, biblical and theological knowledge acquired from books, tapes and videos, even interactive learning by CD-ROM, satellite, or online computer programming—these are all helpful and necessary. But they can't take the place of working alongside the seasoned pros. As Pencom's Jim Sullivan says, "Show-how is better than know-how." And don't forget the best interactive teaching of all: role-modeling followed by role-playing.

If you're a "seasoned pro," how are you sharing your knowledge and skills with others? Do you hold weekly, if not daily, staff meetings? Do you let your staff feel they are a part of what's going on? Do you praise them in front of other staff members? Do you approach your role as trainer from the perspective of a lifetime learner, or as an expert with answers to dispense? Do you accept criticism without taking it personally? Do you train your staff to do jobs other than their own, so their experience is broadened and you will have replacements? Are you individually mentoring anyone? Are you taking full advantage of study leaves (yours and theirs)?

Action: Assemble focus groups of staff and volunteer workers to review and critique all your training methods and materials. Examine content, relevance, and effectiveness. Give the group total freedom to axe and revise the old and introduce and implement the new. Eliminate all training that doesn't stick.

CHAPTER 9

Best Meals, Best Deals

The Cracker Barrel Old Country Store (Bowling Green, Kentucky)

What does it take to entice a family of four to drive past six restaurant billboards on their way to a Cracker Barrel? Or convince a couple to stand in line and wait forty minutes for a table? For ML and me it was the expectation of quality food, good value for price, and dependable, friendly service. Our meal at the Cracker Barrel Old Country Store in Bowling Green, Kentucky (off I-65 at Highway 231), was worth every minute of the wait. In fact, as I said in the preface, "Appetizers," we ate at Cracker Barrels during the next two days of our trip in the Southeast. Why take the chance of being disappointed when you've found a really good thing? The Cracker Barrels do almost everything right.

Restaurants & Institutions magazine also thinks the Cracker Barrel has a really good thing going. Its annual survey of the American dining public found that guests rated the Cracker Barrel the number one family dining chain in the nation—a spot it won by a country mile six years in a row (since 1991). In fact, for several years running, Cracker Barrel swept a field of thirteen family-dining restaurant chains in six of the seven contest categories. The poll rates (1) food quality, (2) menu variety, (3) good value, (4) good service, (5) atmosphere, (6) cleanliness, and (7) convenience (the only attribute Cracker Barrel didn't win).

The 1995 win was a demographic sweep for Cracker Barrel as well; the chain was rated first in all geographic regions, among all age groups, and with both working women and families with children.

Cracker Barrel's motto is "Pleasing People." It shows. Dan W. Evins, founder/president and CEO, says Cracker Barrel's vision is that guests should "get the feeling you have when you finally reach home after a long journey. . . . We want them to be among gentle, kind people . . . in a unique, if brief, visit to a simpler, slower-paced time."

With a light beard, suspenders, and a slightly rounded middle, Evins is a teddy bear kind of guy. His intent eyes twinkle behind narrow-rimmed glasses as he recounts the Cracker Barrel's remarkable rise. In twenty-five years, it grew from a one-of-a-kind country store on the outskirts of bucolic Lebanon, Tennessee, to a flourishing chain of more than 210 restaurants (and more than 300 by 1997). Each year, some 25,000 employees serve upwards of 100 million guests in some thirty-five states.

Back in 1969, Evins was marketing gasoline to travelers. He and a local contractor struck on an idea and scratched their plans in the dirt with a stick. Thus, a gas station that also featured a limited selection of country food was born.

"I wanted to offer a variety of things for weary travelers other than gasoline," Evins recalls. "A friendly place where folks could relax, get a good meal, and browse through unique, interesting, and authentic rural artifacts of a time gone by."

He got the name, he told us, from the old-time custom of holding informal community gatherings in country stores. Large wooden barrels filled with loose crackers were used as tables. Before long, curious travelers were pulling off Interstate 40 to inspect this board-and-batten building and its large front porch filled with wooden cracker barrels and cozy rocking chairs. There, a body could just "set a spell" if he took a notion.

Working on Being the Best There Is

"In that first store," Evins went on with obvious pride,

> customers were delighted to find food you might have found on the table back when your grandmother had you over. Authentic country cooking was the focus of the menu selections and included breakfast items such as juices, eggs, hotcakes, bacon, country ham, sausage, grits, and scratch biscuits and gravy. Lunch and dinner offered simple, but special, country fixin's such as beans, turnip greens and cornbread, steak and biscuits, country ham, sandwiches, and other items prepared in the old Southern tradition. All of the food preparation used authentic recipes time-tested for years in the home kitchens of the Southeast—just as it [does] today.

While the antiques in that first store were for sale, today authentic items remain part of the decor in each Cracker Barrel. But now, reproductions of early American handblown glassware, cast iron cookware, classic children's toys, fancy soaps, handcrafted woodwork, aromatic beeswax candles, and jars of old-fashioned candies and preserves sell in each Cracker Barrel gift shop. A typical store carries 4,500 different items; gift sales account for about 20 percent of the chain's revenues. The Cracker Barrel is the nation's largest retailer of American-made finished crafts. Catalog items are also shipped direct from the Cracker Barrel's automated merchandising distribution center in Lebanon.

"Word got around," Evins continued, recalling what happened in 1969 and 1970. "Folks were telling other folks about the fine food and the atmosphere of this unique little place thirty miles east of Nashville. That's where the waiting lines for that good country cookin' were born and began to grow."

Evins drawled on as we chatted in the Cracker Barrel's modern, wrought-iron-gated corporate headquarters. The facility is set amid lush lawns, ponds, and fountains on the edge of Lebanon. "Folks around here who remember that first Cracker Barrel will tell you it offered good food, a good value, and a friendly down-home atmosphere, and that people seemed to like it." Precisely, I thought as I jotted notes. That's why we were willing to stand in line forty minutes. But if Dan Evins has parlayed a homey roadside store into a corporate giant whose billion-plus dollars of stock is publicly traded on the NASDAQ stock exchange (the symbol is CBRL), he still knows how to sell nostalgia.

The menu has grown, the merchandise has expanded, employee training is extensive and professional. But, as Evins says,

> many of the important things are still remarkably the same. . . . You may not find all the same items . . . you'd have seen twenty-five years ago, but you'll find the same dedication to serving good hearty food. The server's faces are different, but their smiles will tell you if they're glad to see you, just like always. And, just like always, they'll do their best to please you, as if you were a guest in our home for dinner. In a very real way, you are. . . . We're working on being the best there is. . . . But we're still bound by the same

caring traditions. Cracker Barrel's mission is still the same: offering the finest quality and the friendliest service.

In two words, "pleasing people."

Flush Toilets and Satellite Dishes

The old-fashioned look and feel is country: Antiques from the 1890s to 1940s festoon the walls and hang from the rafters. Potbellied stoves, open-hearth wood-burning fireplaces, chess and checkerboard sets for guests to while away the time, well-worn furniture, displays of old-time farming and cooking implements, vintage family portraits: They're all genuine. "But without the outhouse," Evins quips.

Yep, the toilets flush, and the Cracker Barrel restrooms that ML and I visited were immaculate. Guests may indeed relish Cracker Barrel's nostalgic stroll to the "good old days." And their hunger for simpler times may be satisfied through an implicit invitation to a relationship of trust and family values.

In any case, there are less sentimental reasons why people of all ages flock to the Cracker Barrels: Things like the modern conveniences and efficiency, and the restaurant's ability to flex with the times. Unpack the Cracker Barrel and you'll discover the laid-back country image out front is matched by high-tech cutting-edge management in back. Cooking time and portion size are computer-checked for accuracy. Recipes are scientifically kitchen-tested at headquarters before they are sent into the field. Budget, revenue, and inventory information is beamed daily through satellites and computers between each store and the home office.

The headquarters staff includes a full-time environmentalist, and menus are printed with soy ink on recycled paper. (Braille and large-print versions are also available.) A planning task force is hard at work guiding the company into the next century.

Meanwhile, extensive training, a four-level pay incentive program for all employees—and a daunting ten-week stint for would-be managers at the headquarters' management training center—ensure high quality and staff mastery of the Cracker Barrel's rigorous systems and standards. These programs also help keep employee turnover low and morale high, according to O.E. Philpot Jr., Cracker Barrel's vice president of marketing.

In short, the Cracker Barrel Old Country Store has all the makings of a good model for the church of the twenty-first century: doing the traditional, but doing it with excellence, and doing it better than ever before. Adapting, but maintaining an unwavering commitment to enduring value. Cracker Barrel management philosophy blends nicely with the advice of church leadership expert Leith Anderson: Respect the old, but incorporate the best of the new.

Expectations: When you walk into a restaurant, when you walk into a church, you've already formed *impressions* before you ever reach the door: the signs, the buildings, the grounds, the parking lot, the people.

At this point, hopefully, you've been greeted, made to feel welcome, and are about to be seated.

What are your expectations? What are you feeling right now? Are you anxious? Preoccupied? Hurried? Excited? Tired? What are you thinking about? Are you hungry? Do you feel comfortable with those around you? What do you most desire? What do you most want to happen during the next hour? When you leave this place, how do you expect to feel?

Action: Next time you eat out, ask yourself these questions. Next time you go to church, ask yourself the same questions. Mentally or on paper record your answers. Compare the two. Any revelations?

Expectations matter. Service matters. And in church, the theology that is taught matters. In the restaurant business, guests like to be surprised with different, and sometimes novel, food offerings. But they also very much like the security of knowing they can always order again something they have enjoyed before. Some guests sit at the same table every time. Or in the same pew. Consistency. Knowing what to expect. Quality you can count on. These are what most of us want. We are confused by *too much* change. At the same time, we also want *some interest and excitement*, in church and in a restaurant.

So, how do you strike this balance, hold this equilibrium? The Holy Spirit may intervene with surprises even the leaders haven't anticipated or planned. When God is in control—rather than human intermediaries—you can't always program or manage every detail. The one thing you can count on is that there will be things you can't count on—not if the church is the church God intends.

But you *can* prepare the way for that occasionally superlative—even positively outrageous—service that makes guests say, "Awesome!"

This is the kind of service that generates positive, compelling word-of-mouth testimony. This is the kind that far exceeds guests' expectations because the service is unexpected; it involves the guests themselves, and it makes them feel loved by each other and by God. This is the kind of service that causes guests to leave with a smile on their faces and a resolve in their hearts to spread the Word, *tell a friend*. And pretty soon people are standing in line!

One good way to "set the table" for this kind of excellence is to evaluate present performance. I know a newspaper religion columnist who regularly visits churches and synagogues, rating their sermons and services, and publishing his observations and conclusions.

Many restaurants (and a few churches) ask guests for their evaluations. For example, the Mesquite Tree, a small but excellent Arizona lunch and dinner house in tiny Sierra Vista (south of Tucson), hands out "Your Opinion Is Valued" cards to guests. Guests are asked to grade, on a scale of one to five, ambiance, food presentation, food taste and quality, and service. Meanwhile, at Soba, a Pan-Asian eatery in Pittsburgh, partners Tom Baron and Juno Yoon pore over customer comment cards and pick up the phone to deal with some of them personally.

In its annual poll, *Restaurants & Institutions* magazine ranks eating places on (1) food quality, (2) menu variety, (3) good value, (4) good service, (5) atmosphere, (6) cleanliness, and (7) convenience.

Action: Adapt this survey, adding appropriate words (for example, "spiritual" to "food" in number 1, and substituting "activity" for "menu" in number 2), to produce a scale to evaluate your church or ministry performance. Follow up by making appropriate changes—from restrooms to signs, greeters to information booths, sermons to service.

There's quite a difference between *rustic* and *run-down*. Lots of restaurants work hard at looking rustic. None I know of strives to be run-down. Conversely, a few churches are intentionally rustic. A lot are run-down (I've never, however, seen a dilapidated Mormon church building).

A church or ministry structure that's shabby and in disrepair puts me off. Even a sign that needs repainting—particularly a billboard heralding the church's location—tells me the organization lacks pride and is ignoring a most basic way to attract guests. A church in Columbus, Georgia, surveyed its visitors over an eleven-month period and found that a surprising one-third of them were drawn by the church's new changeable message sign.

It doesn't take a whopping budget to replace a sign or trim tall weeds, or, sometimes, even to dispose of an ugly building.

Our gold-country church in Columbia, California, was replacing its aged social hall. The local fire department offered to burn down the fifty-year-old wooden building (to practice controlled burns). Then, session members brainstormed, we'd put up a big meeting tent until a new wing was built. Trouble was, we learned, the old building's attic was infested with bats of an endangered species. So, burning would consume the bats as well—an environmental no-no. We could just picture angry picketers marching around the church on a Sunday morning, placards proclaiming: "Save the Old Bats"! Not exactly the salvation message we favored. So, instead of being torched, Ramont Hall was laboriously torn down by church volunteers, board by board. Birdhouses and feeders fashioned from the scrap wood were sold at an auction to raise funds for the new building.

Moral: There's lots of creative ways to raze a building and raise a budget to work on "being the best there is."

Action: Do some collective brainstorming on low-budget schemes to improve the signs, landscaping, appearance, accessibility, plumbing, heating, and cooling at your gathering place. What could be accomplished through "trade-offs" or in goodwill from community businesses, schools, and agencies? (Don't forget your local Boy Scout groups.)

Speaking of creative ministries, does your church have a gift shop or bookstore on the premises? Would this kind of ministry be a self-supporting or even a contributing segment of your outreach? How about a home page or Web site on the Internet that offers spiritual help on-line, a place where counselors and experts, joined by people with "success stories" to share, could participate in electronic "chat rooms" available in real-time forums accessed by anyone with a personal computer?

In his book, *Starting a Small Restaurant*, Daniel Miller says "Yours should be one of the best places in town to work. . . . Staff is like a family. If it is a happy and prosperous one, many will wish to be adopted into it." This attitude is evident in the high morale and low turnover among staff at the Cracker Barrel restaurants.

The way senior staff—a CEO, pastor, executive—treat supporting staff and volunteer workers determines how they in turn will treat your guests. In other words, healthy staff relations are the key to congregational harmony. And they perpetuate the "caring family" atmosphere and traditions that effective leaders desire to see incorporated into their organizations.

Put bluntly, you can never make your guests or parishioners feel they are a part of God's family if you don't first make your staff feel that way.

I recently spotted a newspaper ad for a Cajun/Creole/Caribbean restaurant called The Palace Café. The headline above a photo of ten beaming white-jacketed workers proclaims: "Presenting ten great reasons to dine at The Palace":

At the Palace Café, our waitstaff works as a carefully orchestrated team. From the moment you walk in the door, you'll be greeted and pampered by ten great individuals who share one common goal—to give you a great dining experience. With our attentive but informal "Team service," each and every member of our staff does their part. . . . Our aim is to provide you with service that is not just the best, but legendary. Working as a team gives us ten times the opportunity to meet our goal. And leaves you with many great reasons to return.

Not just a job: family. A carefully orchestrated team.

What many food workers love most "is the spirit that comes with making and sharing food," according to an article about jobs in the food industry. "That's a camaraderie that goes back to the basics of baking bread together, and you can never run out of things to learn. Work doesn't get much better than that."

Unless it's working together to prepare and serve spiritual food to God's forever family. Here's a three-step program that Jim Sullivan, who leads hospitality training seminars, uses to keep restaurant employees at their peak:

- *Respect* your workers by expecting them to keep improving.
- *Reward* your workers. Improvement follows incentives and recognition.
- *Recognize* your employees.

Churches and ministries can respect their workers by giving them the time and resources to improve their skills and develop their talents. They can reward them through incentives of monetary compensation, time off, and jobs that offer greater challenges and responsibilities—and greater personal satisfaction and recognition. And they can bestow frequent praise on their workers—both privately and publicly—recognizing jobs well done and exemplary service to Christ and his church.

Expectations. Service. Training.

Lots of time-consuming, personal caring, and one-on-one and team training. To paraphrase Sullivan: "But what if you train your workers and they leave?"

"What if you don't—and they stay?"

Action: Train your staff, your teachers, and your officers. Adapt the

"Three R's"—respect, reward, and recognition—to your situation. And pray they'll stay—or else move on and reproduce their skills in an ever-widening and fruitful family circle.

PART 2

Salmonella in the Salad

CHAPTER 10

Strikeouts—and Comebacks

La Torre (Sonora, California); Duke's (Washington, D.C.); Boston Chicken (everywhere); Mission Inn (Riverside, California); Denny's (everywhere)

It was sad. I spotted the full-page ad right there in *The Sonora Union Democrat*:

Auction #3
Complete Liquidation of
Ristorante La Torre
Tuesday June 27th 9 A.M.
39 N. Washington St., Sonora, CA

Everything had to go. Steam tables, ranges, mixer, espresso machine, butcher block, walk-in freezer, tables, chairs, dishes—the works. "All items sold as is, where is."

One of my formerly favorite restaurants—gone. The food and service had seemed so good. The ambiance at this upstairs, downtown Italian eatery was pleasant. And the prices seemed in line.

So what happened? I had already checked out the "Sorry, Closed Until Further Notice" sign that had shuttered the place. Seems that success in the bar killed the restaurant.

Everybody loved to come to La Torre's during the happy hour. Especially on Monday nights to watch football on the big screen television. There were always plenty of free appetizers and heavy hors d'oeuvres available in the spacious lounge. What happened, an insider told me, was that patrons loaded up on the free stuff while they sipped their drinks—and made a meal out of it. They didn't cross the hall into the dining room for dinner. Attendance tanked. La Torre went out of business. No more food, no more drinks. As simple as that.

Maybe they should have required a restaurant receipt as admission to the television lounge. Too many freeloaders, not enough commitment. Like coming to church but leaving before the collection.

Duking It Out

"There is no rejoicing in Washington today," lamented political humorist Art Buchwald. Duke Zeibert's restaurant, a capital attraction since the 1950s, served its last meal on June 30, 1994.

The power elites and Washington insiders dined at Duke's. "The world has been here, I've had royalty here," boasted Mr. Zeibert, who was eighty-three years old at the time of Duke's demise. Indeed, according to *The Wall Street Journal*, seven U.S. presidents from John F. Kennedy to Bill Clinton (except for Ronald Reagan) ate at Duke's while they held office. Mr. Clinton and Senator Bob Dole even had dinner together there to show they could get along. Mikhail Gorbachev, Cable News Network's Larry King, and a host of those who wanted to rub elbows with such celebrities were regulars at Duke's—an "in" place many thought worth waiting in line for.

"You go there for the company," said Ben Bradlee, the former *Washington Post* executive editor, who "Duked it" from the time the restaurant opened until it closed.

But times, like political currents and preferences in Washington, change. Duke's evening business fell off. The rent soared. The opinion was noised around that the pricey American fare—including chicken in a pot and crab cakes—was only mediocre. "Most of it is not very good," sniffed *Washington Post* food critic Phyllis Richman.

So the lease was lost and a Washington institution closed. It was a wonderful place to dine (with the exception of the food).

A church may gain a reputation as an "in" place, too. But if the spiritual food is second-rate, don't expect the guests to keep on coming.

Pecking Away

When Boston Chicken Inc. opened one of its new concept stores in
Manhattan in May of 1995, it was a kind of ending as well as a beginning. Company executives said the opening at 271 West 23rd Street at
Eighth Avenue was a signal that the high-flying restaurant chain had
fully spread its wings—entering the last major market in the country and
completing its major goal of nationwide expansion.

In so doing, the firm plucked the chicken out of its name. Now under the brand name Boston Market, the chain said it wanted to reflect a
broader menu that also featured turkey, ham, and meat loaf.

Boston Chicken/Market took off quickly (standard outlets still go
under the Chicken moniker). The number of its units grew from thirteen
in 1990 to more than 565 five years later. But bigger wasn't necessarily
better. Business at established stores lagged. Competition pecked away
at profits. Hence the Colorado-based management team's decision to
change strategy and expand from its stock-in-trade rotisserie chicken to
complete meals.

Cognizant of subtly evolving tastes, Boston Market wanted to stay
abreast—"relevant to the consumer." That was a feather in Boston's cap,
making it the leading player in the so-called home-meal replacement
category, the growing restaurant segment that offers full fare with more
components than typical fast-food restaurants.

Today's successful entrepreneurs combine old-fashioned courage
and conviction with a rare understanding of the marketplace. Says
Robert Knox, chairman of Prudential Equity Investors Inc.: "They have
taken advantage of new technology, new forms of distribution, and the
changing demographics of the consumer."

Getting there before it's too late. Swinging on strike three and
connecting with a hit. Anticipating needs and tastes. Being willing to
experiment, and if it works, going with the change. And maintaining
steadfast faith in the vision. That's what it takes to stay up to scratch
today, in the worlds of both church and chicken.

Back from the Brink

Like many historic buildings (including many churches and cathedrals), the Mission Inn in Riverside, California, had its heyday—and then a long, slow period of decline.

A date with the wrecking ball seemed a foregone conclusion until a sympathetic—and visionary—group interested in preserving old but usable buildings stepped in. A vigorous revitalization program saved the day: The inn was gradually restored to its original appearance. The style of Old California Spanish Mission architecture—with an international twist that captures the original flavor of the inn's creator, Frank Miller —is alive and well here. The inn, which covers a full block in what was once the heart of Southern California's largest inland city, is a fantasy-land of towers, domes, patios, an ornate gilded chapel, arcades—and even catacombs.

You can almost relive the days when kings, queens, presidents, and Hollywood's most glittering luminaries basked in the inn's lavish beauty, strolled its elaborate inner courtyards, or dined before the cavernous Moorish fireplace. Today, the Mission Inn preserves that unique past.

But the inn is more than a monument to bygone days; it's a lively and thriving part of the present, thanks to those who saw the vision and thought its heritage was worth preserving.

Good advice for church visionaries, too.

Redoing Denny's

Denny's Restaurants had been on the back burner for a long time. The 1,500-unit chain suffered from drabness, sliding customer counts, flat sales, and aggressive competition. Charges of racist policies cost the company $46 million in settlement payouts to black customers and $8.7 million in fees to lawyers.

C. Ronald Petty, Denny's chief operating officer, characterized Denny's as a "forty-year-old concept with no fundamental changes in twenty years."

A major redo of its facilities, image, and attitude was urgently needed. So a face-lift ranged from remodeling to advertisements, menus to uniforms. First, a system-wide pruning: some stores were sold and the rest extensively refurbished. Local ad spending was boosted, and a contract signed with a minority advertising agency to add minority faces. Employees were dismissed or given sensitivity training to root out latent discrimination. And unannounced tests were conducted to make sure each unit had stopped refusing to serve blacks, imposing cover charges on them, or demanding that they pay in advance. The Justice Department called the effort "the largest nationwide program ever to avert future discrimination."

Furthermore, according to a report in *Jet* magazine, Jerome Richardson, chairman of Denny's parent Flagstar Companies of Spartanburg, South Carolina, publicly apologized: "To those customers and potential customers who still doubt us, I say this—please give us another chance to serve you." An agreement was announced with the National Association for the Advancement of Colored People to give blacks a larger slice of Denny's management and franchise ownership. That wasn't all the overhaul in Denny's menu of change.

The Denny's in Los Angeles' predominantly black Watts section began serving soul food like chitterlings, oxtails, collard greens, black-eyed peas, and candied yams as well as Denny's stock items. Some employees started wearing "Denny's N the Hood" apparel. Soon, such popular adaptations served as a model for the entire Denny's chain.

Regionalized menus caught on. The Denny's in the Japantown section of San Francisco now serves dishes popular with Asians. Several Denny's in the Southwest serve Mexican items. And fried okra appears on Southeastern tables.

Sagging sales began to revive.

Resonating with regional and ethnic tastes; offering diverse foods; better preparation and presentation; a new color scheme, furniture, and lighting; attracting new customers without alienating old ones; hiring locally from the neighborhood; minorities given greater voice and decision-making power; dealing with problems in substantive, rather than superficial, ways; not being too proud to admit mistakes and apologize to those wronged: All that brings fresh flavor and zest to tired restaurants. And churches. Sometimes just in time!

---❖---

A maxim in the business world is that you may have the world's best product or service, but if you can't sell it, you've still got it. By not buying what you have to offer, the market puts you out of business—and your misery. Usually very quickly.

In the church, the criteria are a bit different. Yet, far too many congregations and ministries stay in "business" long after they have stopped serving the public. Such organizations often die a slow and painful death. Finally, when people stop coming, the doors have to be closed and staff dismissed.

Throughout *Feeding the Flock* I've emphasized the use of surveys, opinion samples (guest feedback), and evaluation tools to determine your ministry's effectiveness. Some may object that it's hard to measure results "when the rewards are in heaven." True: The ultimate measurement is not of this world. But results *are* a useful measure. They can be obtained through feedback from members and constituent groups, donors and friends—and those who are *not* coming or involved.

Your church boards, denominational agencies, and trustees or directors also need to be assessed, measured, and judged by your organization's goals and mission statement. No group or individual is exempt; none can claim to be outside the accountability loop. This feedback and evaluation is absolutely essential in every area where you have leadership responsibility. Don't accept responsibility without it! If you think you can't afford the time, that's the clearest indication that you must take the time. Now.

Peter Drucker suggests a primary measurement "may be the level of new membership and the church's ability to hold them and keep them coming and becoming more involved as unpaid staff."

When it comes to financing churches and nonprofits, you can't raise money these days by simply declaring a need. Getting a realistic picture of what you can expect from your donor base is helpful. So is getting donors to pledge. Realistic budget-making and year-round stewardship based on sound biblical teaching are essential. But in a time when nonprofit executives talk of "donor or compassion fatigue," your guests' willingness to give is connected to more than their perceived "ability" to donate.

It's tied to their perception that the service they are obtaining or supporting, the "product" or effort they are "buying into," is of value to them. Boomer-age and those younger are less apt to give out of a sense of guilt or in response to a panic appeal of dire need; they are more likely to support a project or ministry they believe in and whose goals and aims they espouse. They will give where their commitment is. Where their heart is, there also will they put their treasure. They need to know what your or church organization does, and what that means to them ("what's in it for me?").

In my opinion, too many churches and ministries embark on major building projects before they are prepared to shoulder the cost. The rationale is that, "once we get this new megaseat sanctuary, once we get twenty-five classrooms, once the million-dollar office complex is in place, *then* the organization will grow and the new members will pay off the loans."

Got it backwards! Wrong strategy!

Even if your building-fund drive successfully elicits the pledges to underwrite it, it may be too great a burden over the longer haul. Remember, as Jim Sullivan says, "great marketing can kill a bad business." Don't invest your time and money to accommodate new guests until your staff is in place and has been thoroughly trained. They need to master the skills and produce the programs that will *keep* those hard-earned guests coming once you've got them! Otherwise, if things go downhill and there's an exodus, who's left holding the (empty) money bag? The "old faithful" remnant, that's who. And they are not going to be happy campers.

Put the money into *training*—not buildings. That's what hospitality management experts advise, and it's true for churches and ministries. Suppose you put just 10 to 20 percent of your projected building or renovation capital funds budget into hiring or training your staff (paid and volunteer). With more ministry, more skills, better service, less waste, and sharper management, your organization will be bulging at the seams. That's inconvenient, true enough. But you'll reap a far higher return on your investment. Let God bring and bless the people first. *Then* there will be plenty of time to do the $500,000 sanctuary face-lift. Train now. Renovate later.

The most important decision you make today won't affect you until tomorrow.

What about the money you've already got in the pot? Seek professional money management and invest wisely and safely. The word is *caution*—you've heard about the nonprofit disasters. When taking over the leadership of a church or ministry in decline or about to fold, here are some questions to ask:

Is the church or ministry in a poor location? How many others like it are in the area? Too many? What are they like? What about parking, traffic, residential and commercial growth patterns? The economy of the area?

What do you know about the previous leadership? What happened and why the turnover? How good were (are) the systems, controls, management, and finances? How large is ongoing debt?

What is the ratio of staff and training budget to capital funds needs? What personnel and equipment are in place? Are the existing services and ministries considered to be of value by the guests and donors? Can existing staff and equipment at least produce the minimum activities and services needed to reverse the decline?

What quality of "spiritual food" has been served lately?

Have the wrong priorities been pushed?

Action: Thoroughly assess the value of a declining or closed church or ministry before determining whether, as its potential leader, you should take it on. Don't play into a repeat of the previous leader's mistakes.

But remember, you are only one part of the larger picture. Teamwork and shared vision will be necessary for success even if you are a highly motivated, multitalented leader. As one person, you cannot assume all the roles necessary to make it on your own. And, as in any venture, there's also the intangible factor of goodwill. It's not included in the purchase price. "God's goodwill" or grace (God's "purchase price") may tip the scale in your decision making.

Here are five basic ways a church or ministry can maximize its outreach and service and avoid declining attendance and falling giving:

- Increase the commitment level (leaders and members).
- Organize outside promotions (in the community and via the media).
- Organize in-house promotions (events within the membership).
- Broaden the "menu" (services and activities).
- Increase the average contribution (tithes and offerings).

Idea: Influence every current guest so that he or she comes to one more service or function a month. If everyone did (and this is an attainable goal), what would this do to overall weekly attendance? Monthly giving? Yearly growth and discipleship? Continuing commitment?

Most restaurants can't be sold easily because the original owner or developer has created such strong individual ties to the establishment that in the minds of the customers, the business and the owner or manager have become all but synonymous. Thus, it's nearly impossible to find someone who wants to take over. In one case, a successful restaurateur did all the cooking and baking, worked the pantry area, and spoke to 95 percent of the guests on a first-name basis—spending nearly a hundred hours a week in the process.

"This business was so demanding," wrote Ray Petteruto in *How to Open and Operate a Restaurant*, "that without his work output and presence, the same quality of consistency that had taken him forty years to develop could not be matched by any of the potential buyers . . . and they realized this."

He didn't delegate. He didn't train a replacement. He and his restaurant were synonymous.

The application to churches and ministries becomes obvious when a dominant popular pastor or leader of long tenure dies or departs and no one is in place to take over. The next batter needs to be warming up, or a strikeout is likely.

Have you had a similar experience in your parish or organization? What problems did it create? Were there positive outcomes? What was the final result? Could anything have been done to share the load or ease the leadership transition? What?

Action: Take steps now to delegate authority and to train staff. Groom leaders so they can assume more responsibility as the work expands. Put a plan in place for the orderly transition of leadership when the present senior official moves on.

In their book, *Competing for the Future*, Hamel and Prahalad identify the inability to escape the past and to invent the future as reasons great companies fail.

What if these inabilities typified your ministry or church? Would you be in deep trouble?

Escaping the Past

Suppose you had:

- An unparalleled track record of success. *Would you then be blinded to the future by your past or present success?*

- No gap between expectations and performance—what happened in the past is all you expect in the future. *Are your expectations exceeding current levels of performance?*

- A contentment with current performance. *Are you content with "business as usual" as the norm, the thinking that goes, "We have always done it this way—why change?"*

- An accumulation of abundant resources. *Are you relying on size alone? Or on the accumulation of members, money, and facilities?*

- A view that resources win out. *Are membership and budget the only indicators of health you measure? Are you combining the records of healthy and unhealthy departments, which can obscure where you are now?*

Inventing the Future

To escape the past and seize opportunities for the future you need:

- An optimized business system. *Are you continually examining your structure and staff in light of your mission and an ever-changing environment?*

- An openness to new rules. *When the rules change, you lose any previous advantage because in a sense, everyone has to start over. Where are you vulnerable if the rules change?*

- To abandon some deeply etched recipes. *Do you expect the same methods and programs that brought you to the present also to work in the future? Are you willing to try some new recipes?*

   Joke:
   Q. How many church members does it take to change a lightbulb?
   A. Whoever said anything about change?

You either constantly move and change with the times or the times change you.

The life cycle of both successful restaurants and successful churches is, at best, short. The Red Lobster and Olive Garden chains totally revitalize each restaurant a minimum of every seven years.

Training, evaluating, and planning ahead are imperative to keep your mission vibrant and relevant. And to better serve your guests and your God, now and in the future.

Are you defending useless old traditions, or are you open to new discoveries? Are you riding dead horses, or breaking bucking broncos?

PART 3

Putting It Together—
Sweet and Sour

CHAPTER 11

The Cracker Barrel Concept

Now that we've toured some twenty restaurants together, perhaps you're stuffed with good food for thought. Time to push back from the table. Let's apply what we've seen, heard, smelled, and tasted.

The Cracker Barrel Old Country Store is, of course, our premier example of why people would sooner stand in line for the food they want than be served sooner the food that is wanting.

I still have the cashier's slip from our first meal at the Nashville Cracker Barrel. On the back, I started a list of all the reasons I could think of for the chain's popularity. When I got home, I expanded the list on a large sheet of paper, placing all the criteria for the restaurants' success on the left-hand side. Then I drew a line down the center and on the right side I wrote parallel criteria for successful church leadership.

Later, in my seminars on church leadership for the twenty-first century, I began to apply the Cracker Barrel success model to church patterns. Using a blackboard or flip chart, I asked my audiences, "What makes a good restaurant?" The list grew as people told about where they liked to eat and why. It was fun—and provocative. "Can you make a parallel between this restaurant and an effective church?" I would continue.

Now it's your turn. What is *your* "restaurant theory" of the church? Think of your favorite place(s) to eat out. List all the things that make this and other restaurants successful and profitable. Then make a church analogy:

Signs of Greatness

What makes a restaurant "successful"? A church?

Based on input from a variety of leadership audiences in several parts of the country, the following composite list and its applications are typical:

Signs of Greatness

**What makes a
restaurant "successful"?**
Good food and lots of it
Good service
Target clientele
People most important
Location and parking
Word of mouth publicity
Advertising
Fair price
Cleanliness
Consistency; quality control
Variety and menu selection
Specialties
Ambiance
"Success" perception

**What makes a
church "successful"?**
The Gospel in depth
Quality; excellence
Determine primary audience
God's people are loved
Location and parking
Word of mouth excitement
Public and community relations
Value felt for time and money
Clean facilities
Certainty and consistency
Choice of attractive programs
Special attractions, events
Attractive, worshipful setting
Activity; "effective" perception

What did you come up with?

Here is another list stemming from my specific evaluation of the Cracker Barrel restaurants and a translation of those attributes to effective contemporary churches:

The "Cracker Barrel 'Church'"
Criteria for Exceptional Effectiveness:

Cracker Barrel restaurants	Contemporary churches
Requires investment and time	Requires investment and time
Requires patience	Requires patience, trust in God's plan
Ambiance	Attractive facilities
Symbols and signs	Symbols and signs
Nostalgia of "good old days"	Remembrance of God's faithfulness
Rural values ("rurbanization")	Respect for nature, creation
Something for everyone	All welcome; Christ calls all people
Well-marked, lighted; high, visibility	Easily found; visible
Adequate parking	Adequate close parking
Cleanliness	Clean and neat premises
Quality you can count on	Consistent excellence
Take-home food packages encouraged	Values that stay with you
Easy access	Easy access; handicapped provisions
Family-oriented	Family-oriented
Reasonable price	Good stewardship emphasized
Good public address system, music	Good sound system, music
Efficient and friendly service	Efficient and friendly programs
Eater-friendly (games and checkers)	Spiritually hungry-friendly
Participatory	Participatory
Warmth (open fire)	Warmth, fire of Holy Spirit
Convenient hours	Convenient multiple services
Adequate staff	Adequate staff
Consistent product	Doctrinally stable, faithful to the Gospel

Rapidly growing in number of outlets	Church planting; missions
Trained management	Trained, competent leaders
Repeat local customers	Faithful members
Attracts travelers who return many times	Seekers keep coming
Plenty of food; large helpings	Rich spiritual food; no skimping
Varied menu with wide selection	Varied full range of activities

If you've been to a Cracker Barrel, can you add items?

Bringing Home the Bacon

Now, here's a different kind of application to try. Dan Evins, Cracker Barrel's president, wrote a letter that was printed on the inside cover of the chain's 1993 gift catalog. What does each thought or concept evoke? What principles is he explicating? How does his letter make you feel about Cracker Barrel Old Country Stores?

Write a word or two in the margin next to each phrase or paragraph that sums up the kernel of Evin's idea.

Then, translate that concept or criterion into "church dialect." How might you rewrite Evin's letter and customize it to reach people interested in spiritual fare? Try doing it; your target audience might like it!

Almost nothing will give you the impression of being inside a beehive so much as watching an old-fashioned country cook getting ready for company. In the hours before the guests arrive, there are hundreds of details that have to be taken care of, and every little thing has to be just so. Nothing is too unimportant to escape the hostess' attention—because nothing makes her happier than to see the appreciative smiles on the faces of her guests.

That's also the sort of spirit that folks have noticed at our Old Country Stores, too. Whether it's opening the door for you when you come in, or taking a few extra moments for a neighborly conversation, or just greeting you with a friendly smile, our people take a lot of pride in seeing that all your needs are met before you even have to ask, just as they would if you had come to their home for Sunday dinner.

But it's only natural that a lot of our guests say they're made to feel almost like family. In a sense, we're a family ourselves: the hostesses and servers and food preparers in our Old Country Stores, and the artists and craftspeople whose products are featured in this catalog. And as a family, we all work together to get ready for company, to make sure that the food is delicious, the whole place is spotless, and your whole experience is perfect.

Whether you're a longtime neighbor or just passing through, we want to provide service that's even beyond your expectations—not just because we want you to come back (we do) but also because our greatest satisfaction comes from seeing to yours. That's why, if you look around next time you're in one of our Old Country Stores, you may notice our people are smiling even during those rare moments when they're not serving anyone. Like the old-fashioned country hostess, they're just happy to see everybody having such a good time.

Sincerely,

Dan W. Evins, President

Here's how I marked up Dan's letter:

old-time values ——
advance planning! —

Almost nothing will give you the impression of being inside a beehive so much as watching an <u>old-fashioned country cook</u> getting ready for company. In the hours <u>before the guests arrive</u>, there are hundreds of details that have to be taken care of, and every little thing has to be just so. Nothing is too unimportant to escape the hostess' attention—

"customer ——
satisfaction"

because <u>nothing makes her happier than to see the appreciative smiles</u> on the faces of her guests.

presence of the Holy Spirit in Church
friendly greeters ——

That's also the sort of <u>spirit</u> that folks have noticed at our <u>Old Country Stores</u>, too. Whether it's <u>opening the door for you</u> when you come in, or taking a <u>few extra moments for a neighborly conversation</u>, or just <u>greeting you</u> with a friendly smile, our people take

meeting needs -
personal ——

a lot of <u>pride in seeing that all your needs are met</u> before you even have to ask, just as they would if you

Sunday service ——

had come to their home for <u>Sunday dinner</u>.

closeness-
family of God
staff is a team ——

But it's only natural that a lot of our guests say they're made to feel almost <u>like family</u>. In a sense, <u>we're a family ourselves</u>: the <u>hostesses</u> and <u>servers</u> and <u>food preparers</u> in our Old Country Stores, and the <u>artists</u> and <u>craftspeople</u> whose products are featured in this catalog. And as a family, we all <u>work together</u> to get ready for company, to make sure that

quality, cleanliness,
value, satisfaction —

the <u>food is delicious</u>, the whole <u>place is spotless</u>, and your whole <u>experience is perfect</u>.

charter member ——
visitor ——
excellence ——

Whether you're a <u>longtime neighbor</u> or just <u>passing through</u>, we want to provide <u>service</u> that's even <u>beyond your expectations</u>—not just because <u>we</u>

return is important —

<u>want you to come back</u> (we do) but also because our greatest <u>satisfaction comes from seeing to yours</u>. That's why, if you look around next time you're in one of our Old Country Stores, you may <u>notice our people</u>

happy, joyful! ——

<u>are smiling</u> even during those rare moments when they're not serving anyone. Like the old-fashioned

Koinonia,
fellowship ——

country hostess, <u>they're just happy to see everybody having such a good time</u>.

from the heart ————————————

<u>Sincerely,</u>
Dan W. Evins, President

CHAPTER 12

Tough Act to Swallow: What Sours a Good Restaurant? Or a Good Church?

A few statistics for comparison: there are about 555,000 restaurants— that is, commercial food-service establishments—in the United States. This adds up to an annual $190 billion business, $148 billion of it in the casual-dining market. But the restaurant turnover rate is 10 to 15 percent a year, and more than half of all new restaurants fail within the first three years.

There are approximately 375,000 church congregations in the United States. One third of them average no more than fifty people at morning worship services, and two-thirds average one hundred or less. Further, 78 to 80 percent of all U.S. churches have either leveled out in attendance, are declining, or are dying, despite amazing growth and vigor in some quarters (among the other 20 percent).

Conclusion: It takes customers/guests/members to keep you in business/ministry. A majority of churches and restaurants go downhill and eventually fail. Why?

I asked a dozen or so experts in the fields of both church growth and restaurant management. Though many reasons exist for failure in each category, I was struck by the similarity of answers. The number one reason in both is *neglect*: not taking proper care of the people you are supposed to be serving.

"It applies to the church," said Don Clinton, owner of seven Clifton's Cafeterias in Southern California and the third generation of his family in the restaurant business. "A successful restaurant is a hospitality industry. Treating a customer like a guest in your own living room sums up the cordiality and warmth and bending over backwards needed to make that experience a good one. That is true, of course, for the church as well."

Direct, a magazine for restaurants, claims restaurants lose 68 percent of their customers "because they perceive you don't care. They believe you are indifferent to their needs and they slip quietly away."

Sometimes they slip away not so quietly. That can be the kiss of death. While positive word-of-mouth is the best promotion a restaurant or a church can get, the reverse—bad word-of-mouth—is deadly and spreads like wildfire. When people feel they are treated badly, says Jim Sullivan, the Denver-based veteran restaurateur, they'll tell ten to twelve other people who weren't there. These twelve will tell six other people, each one tending to embellish the story. These six in turn will tell three more people each. In all, that's *three hundred people* who hear about that bad service experience through negative word-of-mouth "advertising"!

That's a tough act to swallow!

You have probably heard (and experienced) plenty of restaurant horror stories yourself. In my seminars, I ask participants to help me complete a chart that lists what sours a good restaurant. My composite list is growing quite long now, but most of the same deficiencies show up every time. Take a moment and write down the things you think make a restaurant flounder or go belly-up.

Signs of Decline

Here's the composite list I've compiled. How many of your reasons are here? What others did you consider important?

Signs of Decline

What makes a restaurant go downhill or fail?

- Neglect and indifference
- Bad-mouth publicity
- Loss of vision and goals
- Bad food, bad chef
- Poor service
- Bad management
- Boring, dull, no variety
- Low morale, disgruntled staff
- Too little for too much
  (costly—prices not in line
  with perceived value)
- Rancid attitude, rudeness
- Not keeping up with the times
- Changing styles
- Changing neighborhoods
- New ownership (for the worse)
- Competition
- Dropouts, staff turnover
- Stage in life-cycle, momentum loss
- Mergers, acquisitions
- Critics, bad press, media bias
- Dingy, dirty
- Too noisy
- Not trimming fat at the waste line
  (runaway expenses)

Now, write a church analogy to the right of each of your items (or on the above list, if you prefer).

Your comparison might come out something like this:

Signs of Decline

What makes a restaurant fail or go downhill?	What makes a church fail or go downhill?
Neglect and indifference	Neglect and indifference
Bad-mouth publicity	Bad publicity, press; rumors
Loss of vision, goals	Loss of vision, goals
Poor product or food	Little spiritual food, depth
Bad chef; bad management	Pastor, staff inept; malpractice
Boring; dull, no variety	Boring; no variety
Disgruntled employees	Lousy staff morale
Price for value is poor	Not perceived as being of value
Rancid attitude, rudeness	Uncaring attitude, cliquish
Not keeping up with times	Old-fashioned; out-of-date
Changing styles	Leaders out of sync with congregation
Changing neighborhood	Changing neighborhood, location
Ownership change	New leadership lacks ability, vision
Competition	Other churches more attractive
Dropouts; staff turnover	Dropouts; inactives
Stage in life-cycle; momentum loss	Stage in life-cycle; momentum loss
Mergers; acquisitions	Mergers; takeovers
Dingy and dirty	Dingy and dirty
Too noisy	Too much noise, emotionalism
Not trimming fat at waste line	Not staying within budget

Analyzing Faults

Let's look at some of these faults more closely and see what the experts say about them:

• Loss of vision, goals

O.E. Philpot Jr., now retired vice-president of marketing for the Cracker Barrel Old Country Store, says his company tries to keep focused on three things: consistency, quality, and pleasing people. Restaurants go downhill, he says, when they "lose their focus, when they don't care. And when they don't follow the recipe."

Churches decline when parishioners no longer can trust they will find high-quality service—and services—and faithfulness to the Gospel whenever they come. And, as dwindling numbers attest in many churches that have departed from teaching the Scriptures, churches decline when they don't follow "God's recipe." Of course, a church's mission is ultimately to please God and not people, but that can be done by spiritually feeding God's people well.

•   Poor food or service
Cracker Barrel's top management regularly samples the food served in its restaurants, assessing its quality and making sure it comes up to highest standards. "There is," says Philpot, "real accountability" for each local manager. Customer opinion about quality and service is also gathered by exit interviews.

The way restaurant staff handle complaints is the weakest link in customer satisfaction, according to a National Restaurant Association/Gallup Survey. Only 14 percent of restaurants got an excellent rating in that area.

When is the last time your church did a quality check on its "food" and service? And what is done about complaints?

This check could be made through focus groups, staff evaluations, a suggestion box, questionnaires handed out with the bulletins and collected when people leave the building, or via a comprehensive survey drawn up by the staff and lay leaders and mailed to the entire constituency.

Also, complaints need to be taken seriously and passed on to the person or persons who can adequately respond. Recently, a friend of mine wrote a detailed critique of a celebration service that had offended her. She sent the letter to the chair of the Worship Committee. But the chairperson did not share the letter with the music director or even bring it to the attention of the committee for discussion, saying that the music director was "too sensitive" to hear such things.

My friend felt she had not been heard. She said she would have felt better if the committee and music director had wrestled with her problem, even if they subsequently decided not to make any changes in the next celebration.

• Rancid attitude; rudeness; arrogance

Don Riddell, president of a consulting firm for human resources management, says arrogance, or "detachment on the part of management from the customer" will take down a good restaurant faster than a short-order cook can burn a burger.

"The best favor a customer can do for you," adds Riddell, who was an administrator of a cafeteria chain for eleven years, "is tell you when you've done something wrong. Part of being connected to a customer is to create an environment where people will come to you and tell you when they have a problem or complaint."

Riddell, coauthor of a book about building good staff relations in local churches, makes the connection: "This is true for the consumer, and for the parishioner. In the church it's a lack of willingness [on the part of leadership] to listen to what's wrong. An arrogance—'We know better than you what's wrong.' By doing that, you separate yourself from your reason for being there" as the leader.

If you are the senior leader, and your staff is already disgruntled, just try taking this "what's your problem?" attitude. You'll be looking at morale flatter than a fallen souffle!

• Boring, dull, no variety

When the New Jersey Turnpike Authority canceled the Howard Johnson's concession after seventeen years, it explained that the customers had become tired of the food—not because of its awfulness, but because of its *sameness.*

Boring! I suspect that's why a lot of people stop coming to church. Not because it's so awful. It's just that it's always the same. Variety is the spice of exciting places to eat and exciting places to worship God.

But in a sense, there has to be a lot of "sameness"—at least for the staff. Several consultants spoke of "attention to detail." The Lord's Prayer, communion or Mass, following a set ritual or lectionary: No detail, no rubric, can be overlooked or treated in a routine, rote way without losing its freshness and becoming boring.

"Everything is detail," said my cousin Walter McDowell, who handled quality assurance for restaurants and resorts. "It's keeping up on a daily basis. A constant attention. People see this." And for staff, Walt adds, motivation is needed on a daily basis.

To keep the vision on the front burner and deliver consistent excellence, both variety and constant repetition are essential—whether it's serving meals or conducting Bible classes and worship.

• Not keeping up with the times; changing styles; competition
Remember how we saw in earlier chapters that Taco Bell and Boston Chicken (Market) were willing to experiment and try new things, to keep up with trends and make changes before it was too late? Failing to do so in food service or church service is a recipe for disaster. Listen to Randall Parr, writing in *Ministries Today:*

> The best preacher in the world won't get heard if people are put off by the church's public image, the style and condition of the building and the appeal of its programs. Remember, you're trying to reach secular people. If they can't understand your language, they won't be able to accept your message. Put yourself in the unchurched person's shoes, and ask what would convince you to attend your own church.

That's why church and ministry leaders are well advised to keep up with current news, cultural trends, and the entertainment world. Important publications include *Wired* magazine, *Fast Company*, and *Current Thoughts & Trends*. I also recommend *The Wall Street Journal*.

• Bad chef; bad management; ownership change
Francis Lynch, former head of the Culinary Arts program at Columbia Community College in Sonora, California, adds "weak performers in the kitchen" to lack of attention to detail, poor service, and rude treatment of guests as the major reasons why restaurants go downhill. An especially crucial time is when the cooks or owners change.
The parallel to changes in pastoral ministry is obvious. That's the crucial time when "guests" make up their mind whether they'll keep coming—or head for another establishment where they like the "chef" better. Or perhaps they'll follow the old chef to his new place of business, assuming it's close enough and he's not a "weak performer in the kitchen!"

• Changing neighborhood; location
In surveys conducted by research experts, four of five potential locations

for new restaurants are rejected as unsuitable. Accessibility, parking, visibility, safe neighborhoods, reasonable cost—without these key ingredients, the chances of success are significantly diminished. But as we've seen, some restaurants (and churches) thrive despite—or even because of—what would appear to be an unlikely location.

"They'll beat a path to your door if you have the right combination of food and service," avers Don Clinton, the Clifton's Cafeteria chief and a board member of the Salvation Army. Feeding the flock good spiritual food and giving them caring, loving attention will bring God's family into the church fold, too.

• Dingy and dirty

People look for a clean restaurant and a clean church, Clinton believes. "Cleanliness is next to godliness—from the parking lot, to the entry, to the restrooms ... If you [staff] can see, touch, hear, or smell something [unpleasant], so can the guests."

Keeping up on a daily basis. A constant attention to detail, as my cousin says.

• Life-cycles; momentum loss; mergers; acquisitions

Loss of momentum can be dangerous for restaurants—and churches. There's a connection between the fact that more than half of America's restaurants are still independently owned, and that many of the nation's fastest-growing churches are independent congregations not tied to denominational structures. Loss of growth and vitality often occur during a hardening of the corporate—or denominational—arteries. Donald Lundberg calls it "bureaucratitis."

Author of *The Hotel and Restaurant Business*, Lundberg observes that once the corporate chain reaches a certain stage of development, it tends to lose its forward motion:

Entrepreneurs are replaced by professional managers who are more interested in turning wheels than in making the vehicle go in a particular direction. Markets change; fashions change. The bureaucrat in the large chains is more interested in doing what has been done and preserving his own position than in taking risks and innovating. He has position, power, and status. Why should he exert himself unduly?

Lundberg also points to nepotism as a kind of salmonella in the salad:

> The father, who was a driving, driven, capable man, hands over the reins to his son. The son is probably a nicer guy than his father but lacks Dad's motivation. He is secure; he has to prove very little. The organization begins to lose momentum. Not only are sons brought into the organization, but also relatives; and then the old school tie makes its appearance.

B. Carlisle Driggers describes similar struggles to get "the system" changed in the United Methodist Church. (He presented a case study about it at a conference led by management maven Peter Drucker and eminent church consultant Lyle Schaller in the summer of 1994.) "Long-standing and entrenched systems are stronger than those who seek to change them," Driggers concluded.

> They will use the unwitting as well as those who profit from the old system to stop [change]. A pastor questions the use of business principles applied to the church. A layperson objects to the use of different vocabulary. A bishop assumes that a focus on systems is by definition devoid of theological integrity. A board member is afraid that the new effort will take resources away from the "real work of the agency." A denominational administrative agency questions the use of allocations for "something different."

The Main Thing Is Keeping the Main Thing the Main Thing

Ruben Villavicencio is a first-generation Mexican-American who, with his wife, Millie, owns seventeen Millie's Restaurants and several Mexican-food restaurants called The Whole Enchilada. Their company mission statement is: "Our family of employees is dedicated to

1. Making customers feel like valued guests,
2. Serving guests in a loving, caring, quality atmosphere, and
3. Providing good food and value."

"It's not difficult for restaurants to go down," Mr. Villavicencio told me, "when we quit doing the things that please people; when we quit serving them in the manner they need and want to be served. Guests go to a restaurant for food, but also for what people provide for them beyond that. Lonely people come to restaurants. We provide contact with other people to make them feel needed, wanted, and appreciated."

Ruben and Millie tell their workers, "If you don't want to be a servant you're really in the wrong business. Our business is serving others with love; that brings satisfaction and success. Above everything else, we've got to be servants."

What about churches, I asked?

"Churches go awry," Ruben replied, "when they forget their purpose; when they quit preaching the Gospel. We need to give people what they want to hear and what they need to hear. Then, we need to go beyond hearing the Gospel to *doing* the Gospel; only then do we begin to grow and become the men and women Christ would have us be."

PART 4

Thought for Food

CHAPTER 13

Food and the Bible

Jesus spoke often of food. Many of the Gospel stories and parables center around Jesus and hunger, Jesus and feeding multitudes, Jesus and rules of eating and drinking and table fellowship. "Food," writes Leonard I. Sweet, seminary dean and author of *Sweet's SoulCafe*,

> was the language Jesus used to introduce us mortals to the wisdom of God and the ways of creation. Think about it. Every time you turn around in the Scriptures, Jesus is eating and drinking. These feasts are significant. They tell us of a God of joy and celebration, a God of life and health, a God who offers us "soul food," the very "bread of heaven."

The centerpiece of the Last Supper incorporated the common elements of sustenance—food and drink. These, Jesus said as he broke the bread and shared the cup with his disciples, were his very body and blood. They signified his sacrificial death on the cross to atone for their sins—and the sins of the world throughout eternity.

Jesus said: "Take, eat, this is my body, broken for you. . . . This cup is the new covenant in my blood; drink of it, all of you, in remembrance of me."

The Gospel of John records Jesus' words while he was teaching in the synagogue at Capernaum:

> I tell you the truth, unless you eat the flesh of the Son of Man and drink his blood, you have no life in you. Whoever eats my flesh and drinks my blood has eternal life, and I will raise him up at the last day. For my flesh is real food and my blood is real drink. Whoever

eats my flesh and drinks my blood remains in me, and I in him. . . .
This is the bread that came down from heaven. Your forefathers ate
manna and died, but he who feeds on this bread will live forever.
(John 6:53-56, 58)

Although I was aware that food and actions associated with eating
and drinking are frequently mentioned in the Bible, I didn't realize just
how many references there are until I got out my electronic concordance.
The word *food* occurs thirty-two times (New International Version of
the Bible, 1984), often in a spiritual analogy or paradigm.

The word *feed*, appearing in the NIV Bible thirty-four times, often
means to give spiritual instruction or comfort. Jesus' charge to Peter,
"Feed my sheep," contains a double symbolism because it refers to the
care and growth of Jesus' "flock"—his believers and followers. Christians are apt to say that a particularly good sermon "fed me spiritually";
on the other hand, they may say disparagingly, "I didn't get spiritually
fed at that church."

Food Talk Is God Talk

"Food talk in the Bible is God talk," says the Rev. Jeff Smith, the so-
called "frugal gourmet" who is an ordained United Methodist minister
and the denomination's best-known chef. In the Hebrew tradition, bread
symbolized life; wine, joy; oil, fulfillment; and salt, friendship. "Is taste-
less food eaten without salt?" asks an anguished Job, perhaps intimating
that friendship spices up a drab existence (Job 6:6).

Food Offering

Under the Mosaic law, offering meat, grain, and other foods to God on
a burning altar was at the heart of the sacrificial system to atone for sin.
These burnt offerings were to be "an aroma pleasing to the Lord" (Numbers 28:24). Other examples of food offerings in the Old Testament are
found in Leviticus 3:10,11,16; Deuteronomy 12:27; and Malachi 1:7.

The offering of food to idols was strictly forbidden, but after Christ
established the New Covenant and became the once-for-all sacrificial

offering for sin, Paul went to considerable lengths to straighten out confusion over principles of conscience. The fourteenth chapter of Romans and 1 Corinthians 8 and 10 outline how Christians are free to eat food that has been sacrificed to an "idol" because, as Paul says, "We know that an idol is nothing at all in the world and that there is no God but one" (1 Corinthians 8:4).

Yet Paul cautions believers not to use their freedom in any way that could offend the conscience of fellow believers or cause then to stumble: "Therefore, if what I eat causes my brother to fall into sin, I will never eat meat again, so that I will not cause him to fall" (1 Corinthians 8:13). See also Revelation 2:20.

Fasting and Feasting

The words *fast* (refraining from food) and *fasts* occur in the NIV Bible fifty-four times, and the word *fasting* appears twenty-nine times. The spiritual discipline of fasting and self-denial is exercised in order to focus on spiritual matters apart from the distractions of bodily needs and the desires of the flesh. (Is "fast food" an oxymoron?)

Fasting is primarily an individual act, done alone or even secretly (see Matthew 6:17,18). *Feasting* is usually done in the context of a shared meal or "fellowshipping" together with other believers. "Feasting on God's Word" is also set in times of celebration and thanksgiving; often it is in the framework of an abundant harvest season and the sharing of God's blessings. Indeed, since Bible times, when the culture was largely held together by common memory, one of the best ways to hand down culture and heritage was through sharing stories at a common meal.

In those days, to feast with someone was the most intimate thing a person could do. And sometimes it was the best place to get across a controversial message. "Jesus ate with all the wrong people and by that was proclaiming a new coming of the kingdom of God," says "Frugal" Smith, the gourmet Methodist chef.

Bread and Life

Smith, who wears an apron and a clerical collar as he serves up theology on his national television program, laments that bread, once the staple and necessity of life, is now optional. He contends that this makes it difficult for many moderns to fully appreciate biblical language such as the Lord's prayer, "Give us this day our daily bread," or "Lord, unless you feed us, we will die."

While said half in jest, the poetic words of Lord Byron nicely set apart the contrasts:

> *All human history attests*
> *That happiness for man—the hungry sinner—*
> *Since Eve ate apples, much depends on dinner!*
>   (source unknown)

Psalm 104:27 says, "These all look to you [God] to give them their food at the proper time." Other references to God's provision of food include Ecclesiastes 3:13, which says that the gift of God is "that everyone may eat and drink, and find satisfaction in all his toil" (see also Ecclesiastes 5:18 and 8:15); Isaiah 30:23, "The food that comes from the land will be rich and plentiful"; and Ezekiel 18:16, "He ... gives his food to the hungry."

Ezekiel 47 and 48 disclose the prophet's vision of a mighty river along whose banks grow all varieties of trees, producing "food for the workers of the city" (48:18).

Jeremiah 3:15 speaks of feeding in a spiritual sense: "Then I will give you shepherds after My own heart, who will feed you on knowledge and understanding" (NASB).

Down in Egypt Land

The ancient Egyptians had a fair selection of foods, the Bible records: peas, lentils, watermelons, artichokes, lettuce, endive, radishes, onions, garlic, leeks, cucumbers, fats—both vegetable and animal—beef, fish, honey, dates, and dairy products, including milk, cheese, and butter. The children of Israel had all these and more—lamb, figs, pomegranates, olives, and grapes for starters—when they became established in the Promised Land.

In the meantime, during their arduous forty-year journey through the wilderness, they saw plenty of heavenly food—manna—but longed for the old Egyptian fare of leeks, onions, and garlic (Numbers 11:5). Apparently there were no inns with full-service menus along the way. Taverns did exist, however, as early as 1700 B.C. By 512 B.C. there was a public dining place in Egypt. But it took a hundred years more before women could be served in such places (402 B.C.).

The Romans were big on eating out. Archeologists have found the remains of snack bars that once lined the streets of an ancient resort town near Naples; bakeries were just off the courtyard, where grain was milled. By 1200 A.D. cooked food could be bought at cook houses in London, Paris, and other major cities. The coffee house, a forerunner of the modern restaurant, appeared in Oxford in 1650 and in London seven years later. The words "cafe" and "cafeteria" are from the French *cafe*, meaning coffee.

The first restaurant to be called a cafe, according to Donald E. Lundberg, author of *The Hotel and Restaurant Business*, carried this inscription over the door: *Venite ad me omnes qui stomacho laboratoratis et ego restaurabo vos.*

Few Parisians who saw the sign in 1765 could read Latin. If they did, they knew that the proprietor, a Monsieur Boulanger, had written: "Come to me all whose stomachs cry out in anguish and I shall restore you." A pioneer restaurateur's rather worldly parody of Jesus' words from Matthew 11:28, "Come to me, all you who are weary and burdened, and I will give you rest." (Marketing the Gospel?)

Jesus, in his Sermon on the Mount, told his followers not to worry about the menu, asking "What shall we eat?" or "What shall we drink?" The pagans run after all these things, Jesus said, "and your heavenly Father knows that you need them. . . . Seek his kingdom . . . and these things will be given to you as well" (Matthew 6:31-33 and Luke 12:29-31).

"So whether you eat or drink . . . do it all for the glory of God," Paul admonished the Corinthian church (1 Corinthians 10:31). And to the Colossians he wrote: "Therefore do not let anyone judge you by what you eat or drink, or with regard to a religious festival" (Colossians 2:16).

Bread, Fish, and Milk

The well-known episode of Jesus' feeding the five thousand is one of only a few stories included in all four gospels. The point is that Jesus was able to multiply the crowd's insufficient food supply and turn five barley loaves and two small fish into an abundant meal with twelve full baskets of leftovers (Matthew 14:13-21; Mark 6:32-44; Luke 9:12-17 and John 6:5-14). A similar story about Jesus feeding four thousand is found in Matthew 15:32-38.

The word *eat* (and *ate*) appears in Scripture (NIV) 516 times; *drink* appears 321 times. The analogy to spiritual food is clear in a passage like 1 Corinthians 3:2, where the Apostle Paul tells the new, immature Christians at Corinth: "I gave you milk, not solid food, for you were not yet ready for it. Indeed you are still not ready."

And the apostle Peter, encouraging converts in Asia, compares them to "newborn babies": "Crave pure spiritual milk, so that by it you may grow up in your salvation, now that you have tasted that the Lord is good" (1 Peter 2:2,3).

The writer of the Book of Hebrews has a similar message: "Anyone who lives on milk, being still an infant, is not acquainted with the teaching about righteousness. But solid food is for the mature, who by constant use have trained themselves to distinguish good from evil" (Hebrews 5:13-14).

Jesus and the gospel writers often compare physical and spiritual thirst; the word *water* appears in the NIV Bible 496 times. The encounter between Jesus and the Samaritan woman at the well in Sychar is probably the best-known example of the comparison. Jesus tells the woman to draw of the "living water": "Everyone who drinks this water will be thirsty again, but whoever drinks the water I give him will never thirst. Indeed, the water I give him will become in him a spring of water welling up to eternal life" (John 4:13-14). In John 7:38, Jesus amplifies his analogy, saying, "Whoever believes in me ... streams of living water will flow from within him." By this, the Gospel writer adds, Jesus means the Holy Spirit, "whom those who believed in him were later to receive" (verse 39).

When they urge him to "eat something," Jesus tells his disciples he has "food to eat that you know nothing about." When they don't get it, he explains: "My food . . . is to do the will of him who sent me and to finish his work" (John 4:31-34).

The word *hunger* appears in the NIV Bible twenty-two times, and *thirst* appears twenty-five times. "Blessed are those who hunger and thirst for righteousness, for they will be filled," Jesus says in the fourth beatitude of the Sermon on the Mount (Matthew 5:6).

In the colorful description of the consummation of history in the Book of Revelation, the writer speaks about Jesus, the Lamb, enthroned in the center of his people: "Never again will they hunger; never again will they thirst. . . . For the Lamb at the center of the throne will be their shepherd; he will lead them to springs of living water" (Revelation 7:16-17).

And in Revelation 21:6, where the new heaven and new earth are described, the Lord says: "It is done. I am the Alpha and the Omega, the Beginning and the End. To him who is thirsty I will give to drink without cost from the spring of the water of life."

❖

Questions for Discussion

1. Why do you think there are so many references in the Bible to food and actions associated with eating and drinking? Is it because food is so basic to life and growth? Is "food talk in the Bible . . . God talk" as "Frugal Gourmet" Jeff Smith says it is?

2. Do you agree with Leonard Sweet's statement that "food was the language that Jesus used to introduce us . . . to the wisdom of God and the ways of creation"? What is your understanding of "soul food"?

3. Why do you think Jesus prayed over and shared the loaf and the cup at the Last Supper rather than, say, the Passover lamb and herbs or vegetables?

4. Discuss the meaning of the bread and wine as flesh and blood. Is it just symbolism or something more? How would you explain this to someone who thinks this ritual smacks of cannibalism? What was the most significant communion, mass, or eucharist that you ever experienced? Why?

5. How could you make celebration of the Lord's Supper more meaningful in your church? What would happen if you substituted other common food items in place of the bread and wine (or grape juice)? Would that bother you?

6. Have you ever attended a Passover seder (meal)? What impact did it have for you? Do you think Christians should make more use of this ritual? If so, how, when, and where?

7. The idea of eating food that has been sacrificed to an idol sounds rather archaic to most of us who are immersed in American culture today. Are there "idols" to which we sacrifice, though? Can food and drink be among them? Discuss eating and drinking customs and freedom of conscience for the contemporary Christian.

8. Have you ever fasted? For a spiritual or religious purpose? What was the effect? Why is fasting usually done privately? Is there greater impact if a large number of people fast and pray collectively and publicize the event? Should a feast follow a fast?

9. Think of ways you could enhance the spiritual aspects of Thanksgiving and the usual feasting associated with it. Is sharing food with others a spiritual activity? Would you rather (a) give money so food items can be purchased and distributed to the needy; (b) buy or provide the foodstuff yourself; (c) deliver food baskets to the needy; or (d) invite poor or home-less people to join you in your home for a holiday meal?

10. How often do members of your household eat together? Do you use mealtime to hand down culture and family traditions or heritage? Would you agree that to feast with someone is the most intimate thing a person could do (other than having sexual relations)? Have we lost touch with that aspect of meal-sharing that was so important and prevalent in Bible times?

11. Is mealtime the best time and place to get across a controversial message? Announce important news or decisions? Have prayer to-gether? Why or why not?

12. When you pray the words of the Lord's Prayer, "Give us this day our daily bread," do you think about: (a) physical food; (b) having enough income to put food on the table; (c) getting the necessities of life on a daily basis; (d) something else; or (e) nothing?

13. How does having adequate food and drink relate to finding satis-faction in all our toil, as Ecclesiastes 3:13 suggests? ("That everyone may eat and drink, and find satisfaction in all his toil—this is the gift of God.") How is this a gift of God? Do you know those who have plenty to eat and drink but aren't happy with their work? Why? Is labor a gift of God?

14. If God "gives his food to the hungry" (Ezekiel 18:16), why are so many people undernourished and starving? As servants of God, what is our responsibility?

15. Study Ezekiel 47 and 48. What is the source of the river? Why is that important? What happens as it flows outward? What is the purpose of the trees that grow along the river's bank? The trees bear every month of the year—why? Is something supernatural happening here? How would you apply this verse to the work of your church or spiritual group or ministry? Is something supernatural going on there?

16. Why did the children of Israel chafe at being fed manna? Do we get

tired and fed up with "the same old stuff" week after week at church? What would help? (Read Matthew 6:31-33 and Luke 12:29-31.) Do we sometimes forget the source of our blessings, especially when they don't seem exotic enough to suit our tastes?

17. Is it hard "not to worry about the menu"—that is, not to be anxious about what is going to happen in your life tomorrow, or next month, or next year? Is there a remedy? Have you tried it? If so, did it work? Share.

18. What is your interpretation of the stories of Jesus' feeding the five thousand and the four thousand? What was the miracle? If there had been no bread or fish at all, could Jesus still have fed the multitudes? Would he? What application can you make to your church or ministry? What about the leftovers?

19. Do we tend to choke new, immature Christians with too rich a diet of spiritual doctrine, duties, rules, and activities? Or are we more apt to keep new believers on a liquid diet far too long and not give them the solid "meat" they need to grow strong and acquire discernment?

20. Do we constantly need to have two tracks—basic teaching and deeper discipleship—the "milk bar" and the "meat and potatoes training table"? Has your church or ministry addressed these needs? How?

21. How do you interpret Jesus' words about those who receive "living water" from him? What is the inflow? The outflow? Do you know "bubble-up" Christians? What is the source of their "well"? If "living water" is to flow from believers, what is its purpose? Is it anything like the water that nourishes the trees along the riverbank in Ezekiel 47?

22. The symbolism in Revelation 7:16-17 about springs of living water refers to the end of hunger and thirst. What does this mean? How do you square this with Revelation 21:6, where the Lord says, "To him who is thirsty I will give to drink without cost from the spring of the water of life"? What will that be like? Do we think about this very often? Preach about it? Look forward to it? What should we do in the meantime?

CHAPTER 14

Five Great Meals with Jesus

The New Testament tells of at least five great meals with Jesus. They are meals to remember—and to remember him by. Dining out with Jesus combined unusual circumstances, interesting guests, unexpected outcomes, and eternal results.

Let's start with breakfast, the first meal of the day. Never mind that this meal is out of chronological order with the other four that we are considering here; the breakfast barbecue on the beach is the Risen Lord's third appearance to his disciples.

Peter, Thomas (the twin), Nathaniel, the sons of Zebedee, and two other fishermen haul ashore a huge and unexpected catch after Jesus directs them to let down their nets on the other side of the boat. The resurrected Christ then invites them to join him on the beach where he is grilling fish and toasting bread over a charcoal fire.

"Come and have breakfast," he beckons. They wade ashore, tugging at a net heaving with 153 whopping fish. He *serves* them. And in the act of receiving food at Jesus' hands, the disciples *know* it is the Lord (John 21:1-14).

Then there's the meal at Mary and Martha's home, where Jesus praises Mary for sitting at his feet absorbing spiritual wisdom while sister Martha, distracted by all the food preparation, works the kitchen (Luke 10:38-42).

Another meal, a dinner in Bethany, features Jesus (the guest of honor), Martha (serving again), her brother, Lazarus (whom Jesus had raised from the dead), and the Mary with the expensive perfume (she pours it out over Jesus' feet and wipes them with her hair). The house is filled with the lovely fragrance—despite the stink Judas raises over the alleged "waste" of money. Again, Jesus approves, praising Mary's act of love and devotion to him (John 12:1-8).

The Lord's Supper, the central sacrament of the Christian church, was founded on the Passover meal Jesus arranged with his disciples in the Upper Room in Jerusalem. A meal extraordinaire! See Matthew 26:17-30; Mark 14:12-26; Luke 22:7-38; John 13:1-30 (also John 13:31—18:1 for Jesus' discourses to his disciples during the meal), and 1 Corinthians 11:23-34.

Preachers could (and have) devoted a year's sermons to just these passages. In using this book, you may wish to develop a Bible study on the theme of the Passover meal and the communion supper, or Eucharist. For the purposes of this chapter, I'll touch only on the theme of table service.

In Luke's account, after Jesus has shared the bread and the cup with his disciples, he asks, "For who is the greater, the one who is at the table or the one who serves? Is it not the one who is at the table?" The disciples were quarreling over which of them was to be regarded as the greatest. Jesus anticipates the "correct" answer they would give: the greater is the one who is being waited on, the one who can command authority, the one who has the power to get others to do his bidding.

But Jesus' surprising answer to his own question is, "But I am among you as one who serves" (Luke 22:27).

That theme of humble service is also powerfully and convincingly demonstrated in the account of the foot-washing scene at the Passover dinner in the Upper Room (John 13:3-17). Arising after the meal, Jesus strips off his outer clothing and wraps a towel around his waist. In a menial manner that manifests his servant heart, he pours water into a basin. He then washes the disciples' travel-stained feet, one by one, and dries them with the towel.

Peter strenuously objects, considering this an undignified role reversal. Indeed, he says, if Jesus is to wash his feet, he needs to bathe him from head to toe. But the Lord tells Peter: "You do not realize now what I am doing, but later you will understand" (John 13:7).

Wedding Supper of the Lamb

The fifth great meal with Jesus Christ hasn't happened yet, but it is described near the end of the Book of Revelation. All who trust in Christ for salvation and follow him are invited!"Blessed are those who are invited to the wedding supper of the Lamb!" a voice from heaven says to John, who was in exile on the Island of Patmos. Write this message, the angelic messenger continues, "These are the true words of God. . . . Come, gather together for the great supper of God" (Revelation 19:9,17).

But first, before this great marriage supper, comes the judgment. When Christ appears in his glory, all the nations and peoples of the earth will be assembled before him. The great separation will take place. To those on his right hand, the King of kings will say, "Come, you who are blessed by my Father; take your inheritance, the kingdom prepared for you since the creation of the world" (Matthew 25:34).

I think it's highly significant that the great judgment, the division between the "sheep" and the "goats," is based on the words of Jesus that follow next: "For I was hungry and you gave me something to eat, I was thirsty and you gave me something to drink." The Lord enumerates further acts of mercy and kindness: hospitality, clothing the naked, caring for the sick, visiting prisoners (Matthew 25:35-36).

Astonished, the righteous will ask: "Lord, when did we see you hungry and feed you, or thirsty and give you something to drink?" And when did we do all these other things?

The king will reply: "I tell you the truth, whatever you did for one of the least of these brothers of mine, you did for me." The righteous then sit down at the great wedding supper and enter into eternal life. But those on the king's left, who have not provided food for the hungry, drink for the thirsty, or performed the others acts of charity, will be banished to eternal punishment (Matthew 25:37-46).

Feed My Lambs

Now, let's go back to the first great meal with Jesus—the breakfast barbecue on the beach. He has served the disciples. Together in cherished fellowship they have eaten the bread and the fish he prepared. Jesus clears away the scraps. He turns to Simon Peter.

The subject is still food, and the love motivation: "Simon son of John, do you truly love me more than these?"

"Yes, Lord," Peter replies. "You know that I love you."

Jesus says, "Feed my lambs."

He then asks the question a second time: "Simon son of John, do you truly love me?"

Again Peter answers, this time with emphasis: "Yes, Lord, you know that I love you."

The same mandate: "Take care of my sheep."

Still a third time Jesus asks, "Simon son of John, do you love me?"

Peter is hurt, perhaps because the irony has not sunk in. He has not yet realized the correspondence of Jesus' thrice-made query to his own thrice-made denial on the night of their last previous meal together. That was the night Jesus was betrayed, arrested, and turned over to the authorities, the night Peter cursed and publicly disowned his master three times before the rooster crowed at dawn (Matthew 26:33-35, 69-75).

Now, this time, Peter says: "Lord, you know all things; you know that I love you."

Once more comes the piercing, unequivocal command: "Feed my sheep" (John 21:15-17).

When and where do we see God's sheep hungry and thirsty? Isn't it every day in nearly every place we go? What kind of food and drink will we serve them? Will it be the pure milk of God's Word and sound spiritual food? Who would be the greatest among us? Let each one be the servant of the least . . . and the servant of all. Service is love in work clothes.

As Ruben and Millie Villavicencio tell their restaurant workers, "Our business is serving others with love; that brings satisfaction and success. Above everything else, we've got to be servants."

Jesus said, "Feed my lambs."

❖

Questions for Discussion

1. Describe your most memorable meal or dining experience. Did any of these apply: unusual circumstances; interesting guests; unexpected outcomes; eternal results?

2. In the "breakfast barbecue on the beach" (John 21:1-14), the disciples know it is the Lord when Jesus serves them food (verse 12). Why? What is it that makes them realize it is truly Christ? Why do you think that Peter—a career fisherman—counts and reports the tally of 153 large fish?

3. Have there been times when you knew that the Lord was present, that God had acted in a situation or in someone's life (perhaps yours) in such a clear or special manner that the result could be explained in no other way? Share. Have there been times when Christ has blessed you or your church or ministry but you have been slow to recognize his presence and power?

4. What happened after breakfast (John 21:15-17)? Does Christ's challenge to serve and care for others always follow a blessing? Should our service be a natural outgrowth of our abundance?

5. What is the lesson from the meal with Mary and Martha (Luke 10:38-42)? Is it that service can get in the way of discipleship? Or that devotion and spiritual learning are the most important of all? How would dinner have been fixed if *both* Martha and Mary had sat at Jesus' feet? Is there a rhythm between the kitchen and the prayer room? The board room and the sanctuary? Between study and reflection, and work and service?

6. What was Martha's real problem? How can a church or ministry keep a healthy balance between social action, and worship and Bible study, between outreach and evangelism, and the care and feeding of its own members?

7. What is the main point in the story of the dinner party in Bethany (John 12:1-8)? Why do you think the sinful woman (Mary) poured out the expensive perfume on Jesus' feet? Was Judas really concerned about the "waste" of money and the poor? Should a Christian ever give

lavishly, even extravagantly? What if in the world's eyes—i.e., in the prevailing cultural wisdom—the act is "foolish"?

8. Have you ever made a gift (time, money, possessions, talents) that was truly sacrificial? Do you think Jesus "approved"? What does love of God require? Can a church or ministry give in the style of Mary and retain its credibility in the "real" world? Does it matter? How do we actually give something precious to Jesus?

9. Note the different accounts of the Lord's Supper in Matthew 26:17-30; Mark 14:12-26; Luke 22:7-38; John 13:1-18:1, and 1 Corinthians 11:23-34. What aspects of this special meal are unique in each passage?

10. What message is Jesus demonstrating by washing his disciples' feet? Is it a vivid lesson about power and control? Do we fall into the same trap as the disciples arguing over who is the greatest? Do we—only slightly more subtly—base greatness on size, numbers, dollars, facilities, campus, prestige, possessions?

11. Does Jesus' statement, "I am among you as one who serves" (Luke 22:27) apply to churches and ministries? How does this play out in a world that bows before power politics and prominent personalities?

12. Can you handle the "undignified" role reversal of serving, rather than being served, of leading from "weakness," rather than from "strength"? How could you and your coworkers transition to this kind of leadership and service?

13. Is there any condition attached to the invitation to sit down at the great wedding supper of the Lamb at the end of time (Revelation 19:9)? Are we judged by what we believe, or what we do? What is the criterion the Lord will use in making the great judgment (Matthew 25:31-46)?

14. Is Jesus speaking here about physical hunger and thirst? Why are the righteous astonished? Who are the "least of these brothers" today? Where do we encounter them? What do they need—food, drink, clothing, hospitality, care, visitation? Anything else?

15. Food—and the love motivation. These seem to go together in Jesus' commands. How would you apply Jesus' thrice-given command to Peter (John 21:15-17) to your situation in ministry or service? Do you want to be "great"? Do you truly want to feed Jesus' sheep, even if it is costly? Do you think doing so will bring true happiness and reward at that great wedding supper of the Lamb?

PART 5

Just Desserts and Tips

Books

Bergquist, William. *The Postmodern Organization*: *Mastering the Art of Irreversible Change*. San Fancisco: Jossey-Bass, 1995.

Buford, Bob. *Half Time*: *Changing Your Game Plan from Success to Significance*. Grand Rapids, Mich.: Zondervan Publishing House, 1995.

Bugbee, Bruce. *What You Do Best*. Grand Rapids, Mich.: Zondervan Publishing House, 1996.

Cain, Herman. *Leadership is Common Sense*. Denver: Pencom International, 1997.

Callahan, Kennon L. *Building for Effective Mission*. New York: HarperCollins/Torch, 1995.

_____. *Twelve Keys to an Effective Church* (Series). New York: HarperCollins/Torch.

Campolo, Tony. *Can Mainline Denominations Make a Comeback?* Nashville: Judson Press, 1995 (available through Cokesbury).

Drucker, Peter. *Managing the Non Profit Organization*. New York: Harper & Row, 1990.

_____. *The Age of Discontinuity*. New York: Harper & Row, 1995.

Easum, William M. *Sacred Cows Make Gourmet Burgers:Ministry Anytime, Anywhere, by Anyone*. Nashville: Abingdon Press, 1995.

Ford, Kevin. *Jesus for a New Generation*. Westmont, Ill.: Intervarsity Press, 1995.

Goodman, Naomi, Susan Woolhandler, and Robert Marcus. *The Good Book Cookbook*. Grand Rapids, Mich.: Fleming H. Revell/Baker Book House, 1995.

Hendricks, William D. *Exit Interviews: Revealing Stories of Why People Are Leaving the Church*. Chicago: Moody Press, 1995.

Hunter George, III. *How to Reach Secular People*. Nashville: Abingdon Press, 1992.

Hybels, Bill and Lynne. *You Matter to God: The Story and Vision of Willow Creek*. Grand Rapids, Mich.: Zondervan Publishing House, 1995.

Kendrick, Michael. *Supper Club: Creative Ideas for Small-Group Fellowship*. Grand Rapids, Mich.: Fleming H. Revell/Baker Book House, 1994.

Mead, Loren, editor. *The Once and Future Church* (Series). Bethesda, Md.: The Alban Institute, 1992.

Oswald, Roy M., and Speed B. Leas. *The Inviting Church: A Study of New Member Assimilation*. Bethesda, Md.: The Alban Institute, 1987.

Quinn, Robert E. *Deep Change, Discovering the Leader Within*. San Francisco: Jossey-Bass Publishers, 1996.

Schaller, Lyle, editor. *Ministry for the Third Millennium* (series). Nashville: Abingdon Press.

_____. *The Seven-Day-a-Week Church*. Nashville: Abingdon Press, 1992.

_____. *Innovations in Ministry: Models for the 21st Century*. Abingdon Press, 1994.

Scott, Cynthia, and Dennis Jaffe. *Managing Personal Change*. Menlo Park, Calif.: Crisp Publications, 1989.

Shula, Don, and Ken Blanchard. *Everyone's a Coach*. Grand Rapids, Mich.: Zondervan Publishing House, 1995.

Sofield, Loughlan, and Donald H. Kuhn. *The Collaborative Leader: Listening to the Wisdom of God's People*. Nashville: Abingdon Press, 1995 (available through Cokesbury).

Sweet, Leonard. *Faithquakes*. Nashville: Abingdon Press, 1994.

Warren, Rick. *The Purpose-Driven Church: Growth Without Compromising Your Message and Mission*. Grand Rapids, Mich.: Zondervan Publishing House, 1995

Woods, C. Jeff. *User Friendly Evaluation: Improving the Work of Pastors, Programs and Laity*. Bethesda, Md.: The Alban Institute, 1995.

Audiotapes

"Choice Voices for Church Leaders," series by experts on congregational problems (includes "The Best Is Yet to Come," four-part tape series with Leith Anderson and Lyle Schaller), Nashville: Abingdon Press, 1994, 1-800-672-1789.

Videotapes

"Discovering the Future: The Business of Paradigms," with Joel Parker. Charthouse International Learning, 1989, 1-800-328-3789.

"The Inviting and Engaging Church" (series). St. Paul, Minn.: Seraphim Communications, 1995, 1-800-733-3413.

"Leadership is Three Plus Three." Herman Cain. Denver: Pencom International, 1997, 1-800-247-8514.

"The Tides of Change: Riding the Next Wave in Ministry." with Rick Warren. Matthews, N.C.: SpiritVenture Ministries, 1995, 1-704-849-0256.

Newsletters and Journals

American Demographics Magazine. Cowles Business Media, P.O. Box 68, Ithaca, NY 14851, 1-800-828-1133.

The Clergy Journal. Logos Productions, 6160 Carmen Avenue E., Inter Grove Heights, MN 55076, 1-800-328-0200.

Current Thoughts & Trends. The Navigators, 3820 North 30th Street, Colorado Springs, CO 80904, 1-800-288-2028.

Leadership Magazine. Christianity Today. P.O. Box 37056, Boone, IA 50037, 1-800-777-3136.

Net Results. Cokesbury, P.O. Box 801, Nashville, TN 37202-0801, 1-806-762-8094.

Strategies for Today's Leader. The Church Growth Center, P.O. Box 145, Corunna, IN 46730, 1-800-626-8515.

Sweet's SoulCafe. SpiritVenture Ministries, Inc., P.O. Box 3127, Matthews, NC 28105, 1-704-849-0256, svm@leonardsweet.com..

On-Line

Christianity On-Line. On-line service through America On-Line (AOL).

Worship Leaders' Forum and Christian Interactive Network, on-line service through CompuServe. (AOL and CompuServe announced their merger in late 1997, and when the merger is complete, the on-line services of each will be available to customers of both providers.)

Organizations

The Alban Institute. 7315 Wisconsin Avenue, Suite 1250W, Bethesda, MD 20814-3211, 1-800-486-1318. Extensive publications and consulting services.

The Encouraging Word. 23456 Madero Street, Suite 100, Mission Viejo, CA 92691, 1-800-633-8876. Resources for preaching and teaching; purpose-driven approach.

Leadership Network. 2501 Cedar Springs, Suite 200, Dallas, TX 75201, 1-800-765-5323. Publications: *Next*; *Netfax*; *Into Action*; *Starter Kit for Lay Mobilization*. Audiotapes from Leadership Network conferences available through Convention Cassettes, 1-800-776-5454.

National Association of Church Business Administrators. 7001 Grapevine Highway, Suite 324, Fort Worth, TX 76180, 1-817-284-1732. Resource for church budgeting, compensation, policies.

The SEARCH Institute. 700 S. 3rd Street, Suite 210, Minneapolis, MN 55415, 1-612-376-8955. Research on youth and religious education.

Service that Sells. Pencom International, 511 16th Street, Suite 400, Denver, CO 80202, 1-800-247-8514. Training and consulting for sales, service, marketing, management.

Willow Creek Association. Zondervan Church Sources, P.O. Box 668, Holmes, PA 19043, 1-800-876-7335. Resources for preaching, teaching, drama; seeker-driven approach.

Sources for this List

Carol S. Childress, Leadership Network, 2501 Cedar Springs, Suite 200, Dallas, TX 75201.

Russell Chandler, author, *Feeding the Flock: Restaurants and Churches You'd Stand in Line For* (Alban, 1998); *Understanding the New Age* (Zondervan, 1993); *Racing Toward 2001: The Forces Shaping America's Religious Future* (Zondervan, 1992), and *Doomsday: The End of the World—A View through Time* (Servant, 1993). Creative Communications, 698 Hillside Drive, Solvang, CA 93463.